E242
EDUCATION: A SECOND-LEVEL COU

LEARNING FOR ALL

UNIT 6/7
CLASSROOM DIVERSITY

Prepared for the course team by
Will Swann

E242 COURSE READERS

There are two course readers associated with E242; they are:
BOOTH, T., SWANN, W., MASTERTON, M. and POTTS, P. (eds) (1992) *Learning for All 1: curricula for diversity in education*, London, Routledge (**Reader 1**).

BOOTH, T., SWANN, W., MASTERTON, M. and POTTS, P. (eds) (1992) *Learning for All 2: policies for diversity in education*, London, Routledge (**Reader 2**).

TELEVISION PROGRAMMES AND AUDIO-CASSETTES

There are eight TV programmes and two audio-cassettes associated with E242. They are closely integrated into the unit texts and there are no separate TV or cassette notes. However, further information about them may be obtained by writing to Open University Educational Enterprises Ltd, 12 Cofferidge Close, Stony Stratford, Milton Keynes MK11 1BY.

Cover illustration shows a detail from 'Midsummer Common' by Dorothy Bordass

The Open University,
Walton Hall,
Milton Keynes, MK7 6AA.

First published 1992. Reprinted 1993. Second edition 1995. Reprinted 1996

Copyright © 1992 The Open University

All rights reserved. No part of this publication may be reproduced, stored in a retrieval system or transmitted in any form or by any means, without written permission from the publisher or a licence from the Copyright Licensing Agency Limited. Details of such licences (for reprographic reproduction) may be obtained from the Copyright Licensing Agency Ltd of 90 Tottenham Court Road, London, W1P 9HE.

Designed by the Graphic Design Group of The Open University

Typeset by The Open University

Printed in the United Kingdom by Page Bros, Norwich.

ISBN 0 7492 7530 8

This unit forms part of an Open University course; the complete list of units is printed at the end of this book. If you have not enrolled on the course and would like to buy this or other Open University material, please write to Open University Educational Enterprises Ltd, 12 Cofferidge Close, Stony Stratford MK11 1BY, United Kingdom.If you wish to enquire about enrolling as an Open University student, please write to the Admissions Office, The Open University, PO Box 48, Walton Hall, Milton Keynes MK7 6AB, United Kingdom.

2.2

10748C/e242u6-7i2.2

CONTENTS

1	Introduction	5
2	**The spice of life, the soul of pleasure**	6
3	**Learning support**	10
	The arguments for learning support	11
	What makes learning support effective?	17
	The place of withdrawal	17
	What affects in-class support?	20
	Support teachers as change agents	22
	Is support teaching still an 'ambulance service'?	23
	Summary	24
4	**Coping with classroom texts**	25
	How a text can be difficult	26
	Readability formulae	30
	Discourse structure	31
	Solutions	37
	Simplifying texts	37
	Working actively with texts	42
	Diversifying texts	44
	Summary	45
5	**The language of the classroom**	46
	The idea of language deprivation	47
	Power and classroom talk	49
	Shared knowledge and miscommunication	53
	Example 1: Doing what comes naturally	54
	Example 2: Divide and rule?	55
	Example 3: Questions at home and at school	56
	Overcoming miscommunication	58
	A case study: primary science	59
	Summary	61

6	**Diversifying lessons**	62
	Heterogeneous groups, homogeneous teaching	62
	Individualized learning	64
	Diversification	66
	TV3 *Rich Mathematical Activities*	68
	Before the programme	68
	Diversity in practice	71
	Teacher–pupil dialogue	78
	Learning support in a diverse classroom	79
	Summary	82
7	**Collaborative learning**	83
	What is collaboration for?	83
	Peer tutoring	83
	Democracy or economic efficiency?	86
	How can collaboration support learning?	89
	Making thinking explicit	89
	Supporting ideas	90
	Ideas in conflict	91
	Exploratory thinking	93
	Learning together in practice: Cassette Programme 2	93
	Poetry session: extract 1	94
	Poetry session: extract 2	96
	Question-writing session: extract 2	97
	Question-writing session: extract 3	98
	Question-writing session: extract 4	101
	Summary	102
	Barriers to collaboration	103
	Collaborative learning environments	105
	TV4 *The Write to Choose*	108
	Before the programme	108
	Summary	112
8	**Investigations**	112
	Views on in-class support and withdrawal	112
	Difficulties with texts	113
	Classroom dialogue	113
	Collaboration	114
	Using the material	114
	References	115
	Acknowledgements	119
	Appendix: Readability formulae	120

1 INTRODUCTION

1.1 Unit 6/7 is about how we can provide a learning environment in which a wide range of children can learn together. It is planned to take five weeks of study time. So it is really 2.5 units of material. I have organized the material into six sections following this introduction:

- Section 2 is intended as a short and easy opening to the approach in the unit.

- Section 3 is about 'learning support' teachers and the work they do in order to prevent and overcome children's difficulties in learning. There are three readings for this section:

    'Evaluating support teaching' by Susan Hart (Reader 1, Chapter 8)

    'A new role for a support service' by Linda Harland (Reader 1, Chapter 9)

    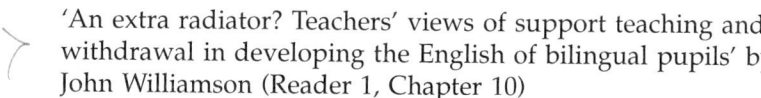
    'An extra radiator? Teachers' views of support teaching and withdrawal in developing the English of bilingual pupils' by John Williamson (Reader 1, Chapter 10)

- Section 4 is about the difficulties created for children by the texts they are expected to use in lessons, and ways round them.

- Section 5 is about the difficulties created for children by the ways in which language is used in lessons, and ways round them. There is one reading for this section:

    'Primary science: starting from children's ideas' by Pamela Wadsworth (Reader 1, Chapter 4)

- Section 6 is about the problems created by the ways lessons are organized, and how they might be organized to respond to the diversity in a class. There is one reading for this section:

    'What will happen if ... ? An active approach to mathematics teaching' by Adrienne Bennett with Honor Williams (Reader 1, Chapter 5)

    You will watch TV3 as part of this section.

- Section 7 is about collaborative learning and how collaboration can help diverse groups of children to learn. There are two readings for this section.

    'Opening doors: learning history through talk' by Chris Morris (Reader 1, Chapter 2)

    'Collaborative classrooms' by Susan Hart (Reader 1, Chapter 1)

    You will listen to Cassette Programme 2 and watch TV4 as part of this section.

I have written the material so that it can be studied in the order set out. It will be easier to make sense of Sections 6 and 7 if you have studied Sections 4 and 5 first. Section 3 could be studied at any stage during the time allotted to this unit. Make sure that you have read the material in Section 6 up to Activity 13 before you watch TV3, and the material in Section 7 up to Activity 17 before you watch TV4. It will help if you record these two TV programmes, to have them to watch again if you need to.

2 THE SPICE OF LIFE, THE SOUL OF PLEASURE

Variety is the soul of pleasure.
(Aphra Behn)

2.1 Here is a list of the 'core problems of children with learning difficulties', taken from a book published in 1990:

- poor retention of ideas;
- a limited vocabulary;
- limited powers of expression, both oral and written;
- limited powers of comprehension;
- lack of spontaneous curiosity;
- an inability to generalize from their observations;
- difficulty in transferring learning from one situation and applying it to another.

(Adapted from Montgomery, 1990, pp. 10–14)

2.2 Now here are some 'slow learners'. Jamie, aged 8, who is described by Mary Caven (1987), joined his new school after being in constant trouble at another school. He found it hard to concentrate or to write for himself:

> He did not seem to care what others thought of him, he often destroyed work you praised, and he was unaffected by peer-group pressure.
>
> It took one and a half terms to discover that he adored 'creepy-crawlies'. So I built a class project around that: 'Beasts and mini-beasts'. It was amazing! He needed to record what he caught, in which traps, for the class terrarium. He needed to note and draw plans of areas where caterpillars, spiders and particularly earwigs

were active in the wild garden. He needed to read. He needed friends to help in the 'nest watch'. Suddenly he wanted to be the class expert ...

Slowly the quality of his work is improving. He is becoming more skilful and acknowledges how useful this is. I am now working on handwriting skills with Jamie. The Insect Club (his idea) needs an extraordinary number of notices, posters and books.

(Caven, 1987, p. 299)

What are Jamie's 'needs': to learn self-control and concentration, and to improve his handwriting? Or to collect and investigate mini-beasts, run the Insect Club and publicize its events? Of course, he does need to concentrate, but this says next to nothing about Jamie. We do not 'concentrate'; we concentrate on something.

2.3 Veronica is a 16-year-old 'remedial writer and reader' in a class who worked with Michael Rosen:

> I told them a story about how when I was in hospital seeing my wife and new born baby boy I had seen a scene where a young black girl in the next-door bed had been waiting for her mum to come and see her and her new born baby. A few minutes later, in came mum and suddenly all hell broke loose, there was shouting and screaming and clearly mum was not pleased. I told the girls that I couldn't really understand what was being said. 'What do you think mum was saying?', I asked.
>
> **Hospital**
>
> Me no wan you, bout man
> soon as me tun me back
> you go pick up man pan you self
> and now you pregnant.
>
> When you come out
> me no want you back a yard again.
>
> Now you come tell me you pregnant
> and you don't even know
> who de fader is.
>
> A wha' wrong with children nowadays
> Dem tink dem no evertytink
> but dem don't.
>
> So you and de baby
> better go fine house
> and live.
>
> (Veronica, quoted in Rosen, 1989, pp. 154–5)

Rosen describes one version of education as the 'jug and mug theory', where the teacher's job is to pour knowledge out of the school's jug, into the child's mug:

> The main problem with this idea of education is that no child *is* an empty mug. Every child, no matter how young, comes to school with 'knowledge' or, as I would prefer to call it, culture. The problem is that unless we ask them questions about this culture we never find out that it exists.
>
> (Rosen, 1989, p. 15)

2.4 Sean, a Year 8 pupil, is said to have severe problems with writing. He wrote a story which is discussed by Gervase Phinn (1987). It is shown in Figure 1.

How would you assess this story? We could take it as evidence of his spelling problems. He has spelt many words correctly: 'incredible', 'locked', 'purplish', 'place'; but he has spelt many words incorrectly as well. His misspellings reveal systematic attempts to apply sound–letter correspondences: 'looze', 'obzirvatry', 'corije'; he knows about many spelling patterns, such as –tion in 'poshtoin', even if he has the letters out of order. There is lots to praise and lots to work on. But is this all we can say? How would you feel if your tutor returned your first TMA with nothing but criticism (positive and supportive, of course) on your grammar, punctuation, paragraphing and handwriting? Wouldn't you expect a response to your ideas – to the meaning of what you had written? Couldn't Sean expect the same? His story (based on *The Incredible Hulk*) is a tale of dilemma, folly and redeeming sacrifice. Sean is coming to terms with tragedy, where people become trapped in lethal webs of their own making. The doctor is caught between a patient 'groning terebly' and his uncertainty about the new potion: he 'just had to hope'. But the doctor's fear for his job leads to fear for his life. As the stakes are raised, so the doctor's self-interest gives way to altruism. He is no selfless cardboard hero though: 'it was the only way to keep a lot of people alive maybe even hiself'. The irretrievable act of giving the potion and the emotions behind it are tightly conveyed: 'he put up his corije and did it'. Motive, emotion and action are powerfully intertwined. Dramatic tension develops through the narrative; after critical events come tense pauses, either filled with a telling detail: 'The mixture formed a little dribble down the front of his lips', or left empty: 'Then there was silence'. Is Sean a careless writer? A poor speller? Or a spinner of breathless, gripping tales?

2.5 Our propensity to see the resources, interests and achievements of children and young people, as opposed to their failures and deficits, depends on a willingness to see them as something other than approximations to a common standard. In special education there is a tendency for children who experience difficulties to be seen as versions of a common deficient type. To do so is to lose a great deal of valuable information about children and how they can be helped to learn. Jamie, Veronica and Sean are all making committed efforts to grapple with experiences, to extract order and meaning from them, to express them through the practices of our, and their, culture: science, mathematics, advertising, poetry, narrative. They defy most stereotypes of 'slow learners'. Their efforts are the spice of life, the soul of pleasure. This unit is about how we might help them and others to make those efforts.

The incredible man.

One day there was a Docter. He was trying his new poshtoin on a man. It was sticky purplish green the poshoin was. The man was very poly. He was groning terebly. So Docter dearion just had to hope that the sticky poshtoin would work. It was a hard situation for Docter Dearion. Because if it didn't work he would looze his job. Anyway he put up his corije and did it. The mixture fomed a little drible down the front of his lips. Then a tereble thing hopend. The man went pale and stared at the Docter. He grow into a masive size and then his myslelses grow terebly big. He grouled. Docter Dairion fled out of his obzirvatry and locked the door after him. and when he had done the so the door flung open. And in its place stood the incredible man. He said what have you done to me. He shaked the place with his loud voice. And he shaked docter Dearion aswell. I have gave you some of my poshoin and it must of erected you a lot I know it has said the incredible man then there was silance Docter Dearion thoarght it carn't be. Then the Incredible man said you stupid fooll and walked slowly towards docter Dearion and gave punch and amed at Docter Dearon and mrsed he made a masive hole in the wall. Then Docter dearion fled in to his room and he drank some of the poshion it was the only way to keep a lot of people alive maybe even hrself and on the same thing hopend to himself.

They fort the day though the Incredible men did. untill they killed each other.

Figure 1   *John's story: the incredible man*

3 LEARNING SUPPORT

3.1 Learning support teachers are specially charged with preventing and overcoming difficulties in learning. They are a varied collection of people with varied jobs, as you can see from these snippets from days in the life of learning support teachers in ordinary schools, all taken from Booth, Potts and Swann (1987):

Muriel Adams, a remedial teacher in Grampian

There we were in the corridor, the boys and I, estimating then measuring a hop, a jump forward, a jump backwards, a bunny jump. A bunny jump? 'Miss! What's a bunny jump?' Well! Sometimes actions do speak louder than words and so there followed the *modus operandi* demonstrated by myself (appropriately clad, I'm glad to say) observed in stunned silence but, to their credit, with not even the merest hint of a suppressed giggle, by my gang of four, and only briefly interrupted by the even more than usually ubiquitous janitor and one passing parent (pp. 169–70).

June, a secondary learning support teacher

Some of the best cooperative teaching I ever did was in biology, and what I know about biology you could write on the back of a stamp, because I never did it. I could see very clearly where the kids didn't understand because it was where I didn't understand either (p. 186).

Paul, a secondary learning support teacher

I know this sounds terribly devious, but it may be that the teacher has asked you in in order to keep Willie and Jeannie and Annie quiet and busy [and] out of their hair, but you say, well I can come in for *x* weeks, or I will do it pro tem, and what you're really trying to judge is when have I established enough credibility to be able to say, 'Don't you think it would be good if we sat down *before* the lesson next week?' … (p. 185).

3.2 In Unit 1/2 you read an account of the development of learning support in Whitmore School (Reader 2, Chapter 2) and you saw how support for children with disabilities is provided at The Grove School (TV1 and Reader 2, Chapter 1). The changes in both schools involved the introduction of in-class support. In this section I am going to examine the issues that lay behind these changes, and to set them in a broader context. In the 1980s across the UK there was a move away from providing remedial education by withdrawing pupils from the mainstream curriculum. What were the arguments behind this move?

Christine Gilbert and Michael Hart summarize the arguments at Whitmore School in three points:

- in-class support would tackle the problems pupils actually faced in mainstream classrooms;
- it would aid communication between class and support teachers, helping them to coordinate their efforts;
- it would break down the belief that most pupils could cope with lessons and only a very few needed to be singled out for extra help.

Were the arguments the same in other schools and LEAs? What issues and problems have schools and teachers had to tackle in the process of developing in-class support? What range of practices have emerged under the banner of 'learning support'? These are the issues I shall discuss in this section.

THE ARGUMENTS FOR LEARNING SUPPORT

3.3 In 1986 the journal *Remedial Education* changed its name to *Support for Learning*. This was one sign of the changes in the 1980s in the way schools and LEAs responded to pupils who experience difficulties in learning. In the years running up to the publication of the Warnock Report in 1978 (DES, 1978), and the 1981 Education Act, many primary and secondary schools took the view that the best way to deal with children with learning difficulties was to remove them from the mainstream curriculum. Their removal lasted for varying amounts of time. In some cases, it was total and long-term: children were placed in separate remedial classes to be taught by one or a small number of remedial teachers for most or all of their curriculum. In other cases, children were withdrawn from mainstream lessons for short periods of the timetable. During this time they would be given lessons individually or in a small group. Withdrawal teaching was predominantly aimed at improving pupils' literacy so they could cope with the demands of the rest of the curriculum, although in some cases it also involved work on basic numeracy and other areas as well. This approach has come to be known as 'traditional' remedial education. In the 1970s, in-class support was rare. Equally uncommon was the idea that specialist teachers should work with mainstream teachers advising and offering materials for pupils with learning difficulties, but should not actually teach any children themselves. But by the early 1980s substantial changes were under way across the UK. At least, changes were under way in what people said ought to happen, in the image of practice conveyed by the professional literature, and in some schools. A broader picture of current practice is harder to get at.

3.4 Two large-scale surveys give us a picture of practice across the country at that time. Gipps, Gross and Goldstein (1987) surveyed provision for pupils with learning difficulties in English and Welsh LEAs in 1983. They asked LEAs what forms of provision for learning difficulties they knew of in their schools. Table 1 shows their results. These figures don't tell us exactly how widespread each form of provision was, but they indicate that by this stage separate full-time remedial classes were becoming uncommon. Withdrawal was frequently used, as were special programmes for individual pupils conducted in mainstream classrooms. Information about the state of play in secondary schools at the start of the 1980s comes from a study of a fifth of secondary schools in England and Wales by Clunies-Ross and Wimhurst (1983). Most of the schools used a combination of approaches. 55 per cent had separate, full-time 'slow learner classes', which were twice as common in Years 7–9 as in Years 10 and 11. 73 per cent had subject-specific sets for pupils with learning difficulties. 52 per cent offered options specifically for pupils with learning difficulties, generally in Years 10 and 11. 85 per cent used withdrawal for individual or small-group work, most commonly done with pupils in Years 7–9. But only 13 per cent used any other approaches, including in-class support.

Table 1   Provision for pupils with learning difficulties in primary schools, 1983.

Type of provision in primary schools	Percentage of LEAs in England and Wales who were aware of this type in some of their schools, 1983
Full-time remedial classes outside ordinary schools, for example, in progress centre	17
Full-time remedial classes in ordinary schools	41
Part-time withdrawal to groups *outside* ordinary schools	47
Part-time withdrawal to groups *within* the school	90
Special programmes for individual children in ordinary classrooms	77
Support to the teacher via advisory teachers, advisers, etc.	87

(Source: Gipps, Gross and Goldstein, 1987, p. 43)

3.5   Writing in 1991, I do not know exactly how the picture has changed nationally. However, I can be quite certain that separate remedial classes are now rare, withdrawal is less common, support teaching in mainstream lessons is much more common, and support teachers now spend much more of their time supporting teachers and curricula, as against individual pupils, than they used to. But the changes have happened at different rates in different parts of the country. Whitmore School shows the extent of the changes in the 1980s in some schools. I don't know what provision will look like in your school, or your area, as you read this. Do you? If not, you might wish to find out.

3.6 What brought about the changes during the 1980s? What arguments led away from separate remedial classes and withdrawal, towards what we now commonly call 'support teaching'? These arguments are not just of historical interest. They continue to shape the debate about learning difficulties in school.

Activity 1 Withdrawal and in-class support: for and against

Write down as many reasons as you can think of for and against two ways of providing for pupils who experience difficulties in learning in school:

(a) withdrawing them for specialist teaching, and

(b) supporting them by working cooperatively with class/subject teachers in mainstream lessons. (The account of practice at Whitmore School (Reader 2, Chapter 2) contains several reasons favouring cooperative teaching.)

These two types of provision cover many practices. If your immediate response is: 'it depends what you mean by ... ' then write down the finer distinctions you want to make within each type of provision and press on with the activity. It's intended to prime you to study the first two readings in this double unit, comparing your own position with the views expressed there. Later on we shall explore exactly what withdrawal and support teaching might involve.

3.7 In the move away from 'traditional' remedial education, Scotland was ahead of the rest of the UK, prompted by an important report by Scottish HMI (SED, 1978), mentioned in Reader 2, Chapter 2. In the late 1970s, the response to learning difficulties in most Scottish primary and secondary schools was to withdraw pupils for specialist teaching in literacy and numeracy skills. The report advanced several arguments against this approach:

- There were more pupils experiencing difficulties in mainstream lessons than could ever be helped by the available remedial teachers. Withdrawing only a few of them was an inefficient use of remedial teachers' expertise, which ought to be more widely available (at Whitmore School, help was extended to pupils making rapid progress as well).

- The curriculum of pupils who were withdrawn was restricted and sometimes monotonous, and could deny children other activities in which they might find enjoyment and success.

- In withdrawal work, children typically acquired and practised mechanical skills of reading and writing, but this did not help them to use these skills in the mainstream classroom: 'drilling pupils in routine exercises, usually in isolation from a context which meant something to them, does not itself assist them to move from mechanical competence to a real grasp of reading, composition, or computation' (SED, 1978, p. 24).

- Time spent in withdrawal work meant time missed in mainstream lessons. Pupils returning to their lessons were expected to pick up the threads, with little opportunity to catch up on what they had missed.

- Work done in remedial lessons might be quite unconnected with the rest of the timetable, and might not address the problems that pupils had in coping with the demands of mainstream lessons.

- Many of the difficulties pupils encountered in mainstream lessons 'stem from the fact that they are having to tackle work which is not suitable for them' (SED, 1978, p. 23). In other words, the problem lay in the curriculum, and withdrawal made no contribution to its solution.

3.8 All these arguments led Scottish HMI to the conclusion that the very idea of 'remedial education' was misplaced. The focus of attention was wrong: 'We believe that the proper approach to the problem lies through the whole curriculum. We have implied throughout that *appropriate, rather than remedial, education* is required' (SED, 1978, p. 31, my emphasis). In an influential paper of the same period, Golby and Gulliver (1979) described remedial education as an 'ambulance service' for an accident-prone curriculum. The task, they said, should not be to keep the ambulances running, but should be to reduce the risk of accidents by changing the curriculum so that it limited the casualties it caused. Many of the changes in learning support since then have been based on this aim of more fundamental curriculum reform. In reviewing the way schools provide learning support now we need to consider how far it has been achieved.

3.9 Another argument against traditional remedial education concerned the question of who had, and who should have, the skills and expertise to teach pupils who experience difficulties in learning. Ingrid Lunt (1987) argued that one effect of withdrawal is:

> the professional deskilling or lack of expertise implied by the referral out. It is as though the teacher might say, 'I was trained to teach normal children. This one has special educational needs, is maladjusted, has a specific learning difficulty, etc., and I do not have the expertise necessary to teach him'.
> (p. 111)

Not only might withdrawal maintain such mistaken beliefs, but it would also fail to give mainstream teachers any expertise that they might actually need. It could also reinforce an erroneous view that pupils who experience difficulties in learning need distinctly specialist teaching. Whether support teaching always succeeds in correcting these problems is a matter which I shall take up shortly. Staff at Whitmore School argued that in-class support did more than just give mainstream teachers a sense of responsibility for all pupils; it could offer reassurance for otherwise isolated teachers who were unsure about their practice. It also offered opportunities to improve teaching through joint planning, teaching, assessment and evaluation (see Reader 2, Chapter 2, Table 4). In sum, two heads are better than one.

3.10   In some schools, services for children with learning difficulties were fragmented and uncoordinated. The opportunity to change from traditional remedial practice to learning support was also a chance to integrate these services. Whitmore School integrated three support departments as well as establishing in-class support. It is still common to have more than one department providing services for children with special needs in the same school, each operating independently of the other. Later in the course, when you watch TV8 you will see some of the work of a department for children with visual disabilities in a comprehensive school. The same school has a learning support department which works quite separately.

3.11   The arguments so far all concern the curriculum and the way schools organize their staff. There were other arguments as well. Withdrawing children for separate remedial education, it was claimed, identified and stigmatized a distinct group of pupils as failures. This could have several consequences. Withdrawn pupils might be devalued by their teachers and peers as a result of being singled out for special attention. This is part of the process referred to as 'labelling'. According to this view, children are evaluated on the basis of their status as 'remedial pupils' rather than on the basis of their actual abilities. This would then affect the labelled pupils' views of themselves and their relationship to their school. Pupils labelled as failures would come to have a poor opinion of themselves and would believe themselves to be incompetent. The expectations of others would produce a 'self-fulfilling prophecy' (Rosenthal and Jacobsen, 1968). Such pupils, it was argued, would also be vulnerable to recruitment into an 'anti-school subculture', created as a defence against the insult to pupils' sense of self-worth which school presented (Hargreaves, 1967; Davies, 1980; Woods, 1980). Labelling and stigmatization are sometimes described as 'social consequences' of selection for a separate curriculum, but the argument points to damaging effects for the intellectual experience of labelled pupils as well. This was one reason why the maths department at Whitmore School changed its curriculum (see Reader 2, Chapter 2, Section 4).

3.12   Ron Best (1987) investigated the ways in which selection for remedial education affected the social position of pupils in two comprehensive schools. In 'School A', teachers who worked with pupils with learning difficulties were called the 'basic skills staff'. They worked mainly with small, stable, bottom-stream classes for English, maths and communication skills. In 'School B' there was a 'supportive education' department. The staff worked mainly alongside subject teachers in mainstream lessons. They also offered 20-minute workshops in specific skills – mainly literacy and numeracy – for two or three pupils at a time.

Both schools had changed the name of their support department – School B changed its organization as well – to avoid the dangers of stigmatization and labelling. Best interviewed small groups of pupils in both schools about their perceptions of other pupils who received help from learning support staff. He concluded:

> Despite the stated philosophy of the departments in both schools – and in the case of School B, of the official overall school policy – and despite some pupils' descriptions of 'teasing' of a fairly innocuous nature, in both schools identification with the work of the 'remedial' department can lead to prolonged and painful labelling and stigmatization of the individual ... The degree to which one is subjected to it seems to be a function of (*inter alia*) the frequency and duration of one's association with the department. Thus, children who attend only for a few 'workshops' of twenty minutes or so over a period of a few weeks do not seem to be subjected to the same treatment as those who are in a permanent 'remedial' group or who have 'gone to Mr B.' regularly for years. The degree of stigma resulting from association with the specialist department may also be affected by who you are and who else uses this service: if children who are popular and known to be able are also seen to avail themselves of assistance with (say) spelling, then other clients are less likely to be despised. Indeed, a useful distinction here would seem to be one between the 'casual' and the 'regular' user of the department.
>
> It follows from the foregoing discussion, that the School B model might be seen as heading in the right direction if the avoidance of stigma is the prime objective. By 'floating' in ordinary classes where even the 'brightest' child may be observed to receive assistance, and by holding workshops in a variety of skills, and open to any (including the 'most able'), the distinction between the 'regular', 'casual' and 'non-user' of the department fades. It is arguable, therefore, that the school is creating a climate of observed experience in which the incidence of victimization is minimized. However, even here we observed an unacceptable level of torment for particular individuals.
>
> (Best, 1987, pp. 94–5)

We shall take a more detailed and critical look at labelling and self-fulfilling prophecies in Units 10 and 11/12.

WHAT MAKES LEARNING SUPPORT EFFECTIVE?

Activity 2   Withdrawal and in-class support: a closer look

Now read 'An extra radiator? Teachers' views of support teaching and withdrawal in developing the English of bilingual pupils' by John Williamson (Reader 1, Chapter 10).

We might conclude from the arguments against separate remedial education that withdrawal is 'a bad thing' and in-class support 'a good thing'. But would this general conclusion be valid? In the first reading for this unit, John Williamson looks in more detail at the arguments on both sides. He does so from a slightly different perspective, since the chapter is based on the views of teachers who support children whose learning difficulties arise from the fact that English is not their first language. The arguments are essentially the same as those for native English speakers who experience difficulties in learning. (What does this mean for the way we define learning difficulties?) At Whitmore School the Learning Support Department included the formerly separate remedial and ESL (English as a Second Language) teachers.

You will find that the points in this chapter come thick and fast. It will help to compile a list of the arguments in each section. When you have finished:

(a) make a list of the circumstances under which withdrawal might be part of a wider learning support system which includes cooperative teaching and in-class support;

(b) make a list of the factors that affect the value of in-class support.

The place of withdrawal

3.13   Surveys of the views of primary class teachers (Gipps *et al.*, 1987; Richmond and Smith, 1990) have found that regular withdrawal work remains a popular strategy for supporting pupils with learning difficulties. But the rationale that teachers give for withdrawing children varies widely. Some adhere to a view of learning difficulties criticized by Scottish HMI:

> Withdrawal teaching can help a great deal. Only a small number of children find classroom work difficult. They need specialist teaching that classroom teachers do not feel confident about.
>
> (Primary teacher quoted in Richmond and Smith, 1990, pp. 304–5)

3.14   Others have found a place for small-group withdrawal work as part of a wider support system. Withdrawal need not mean a rejection by the mainstream teacher of responsibility for certain parts of certain children's curricula. On the contrary, it can be part of a jointly planned strategy for meeting the needs of all pupils. In Unit 1/2 you read the

A day in the life of a support teacher ...

Norma Forsberg, Head of Special Needs at Harold Hill Community School

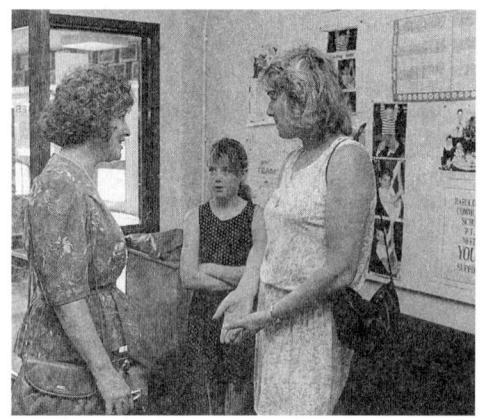

9.30 a.m.   A new intake pupil arrives for an interview with her future form tutor – me.

10.30 a.m.   An impromptu meeting of special needs staff on the stairs to swap information, before I go on breaktime duty.

11.15 a.m.   In-class support: GCSE Year 10 English lesson in the information technology area.

1.15 p.m.   Contacting an outside agency in a spare moment.

1.20 p.m. Annual review of a statemented pupil – checking the completed rough draft with the statementing teacher.

1.35 p.m. In-class support in a Year 7 maths lesson.

2.40 p.m. In the staffroom, snatching a cup of coffee before driving to the school's other site ('centre'), I hear more information about a pupil.

3.00 p.m. Special Needs Departmental meeting, across centres – discussion on whole-school issues.

views of Helen Matthews (1987), a support teacher in the Grampian Region. She argues that decisions on whether to withdraw should depend on exactly what the task is, how it relates to the rest of the curriculum and what the best setting for support on this task is. She advocates withdrawal for specific short-term purposes. Her approach is similar to the short workshops in Ron Best's School B. One of the arguments against withdrawal is the stigma it creates. But if withdrawal for a variety of purposes is a normal part of classroom life for many pupils, then it is less readily associated with low status.

What affects in-class support?

3.15 The teachers interviewed by Williamson identified several aspects of in-class support which could alter its effectiveness:

(a) *The degree of joint planning between mainstream and support teacher.*

One of the greatest barriers to joint planning is a straightforward lack of time. If no joint planning is possible, how valuable is in-class support?

(b) *The mainstream teacher's methods.*

Support teachers have sometimes found themselves propping up lessons that were not effective for any pupils in the class (Best, 1991; Hart, 1987). Ron Best calls support teachers working in mainstream lessons 'floaters':

> If the floater is supporting the learning of false facts, confusing concepts or useless skills, then her/his time is hardly well spent ... Ironically, the role of the support teacher as floater may be easier, and apparently more 'effective', in lessons whose educative quality is dubious, precisely because the purpose and nature of the activities are not apparent to pupils. I was in great demand in lessons using worksheet exercises in formal grammar divorced from a meaningful context.
>
> (Best, 1991, p. 28)

(c) *The level of agreement between the two teachers about what learning support is for and how it should be provided.*

In Richmond and Smith's (1990) survey many primary teachers saw cooperative teaching in mainstream lessons as another way to deliver individual tuition in basic literacy skills. They did not see support teaching as trying to change the curriculum, yet their LEA's policy favoured this approach.

(d) *The support teacher's knowledge of the subject, materials and methods of the lesson.*

Some departments in some secondary schools take the view that an in-depth knowledge of the subject matter of a lesson is essential for effective learning support. In TV4, which you will watch as part of this double unit, the comprehensive school maths department where we filmed used learning support, but from its own staff, not from the school's learning support department. How much do you need to know to offer effective support? How this question was handled at Whitmore School is discussed in Reader 2, Chapter 2, Section 2.

(e) *The support teachers' skill and confidence in suggesting changes to the mainstream teacher.*

One of the roles that support teachers in Scotland began to take on after the HMI Report was 'consultant' to mainstream teachers. Whether you can be an effective consultant depends on whether you have relevant expertise to offer and the sensitivity to convey it without offending people (Booth, 1987). Training courses for support teachers often include material on the social skills of effective collaboration. Dyer (1988) captures the personal difficulties inherent in the role:

> If I tell you that you are doing a great job, I may say that I am supporting you. On the other hand, grateful for my words, you may nevertheless feel that my deeds do not match them and complain that I am giving you no support whatsoever. Stung by realization, I might come into your classroom in my capacity as a support teacher only to find that what I thought of as support appeared to you to be intrusion.
> (Dyer, 1988, pp. 6–7)

(f) *The way in which the two teachers share classroom management and discipline.*

One of the occupational hazards of support teachers working with several mainstream teachers is a form of pedagogic schizophrenia. They have to adopt different styles in different classrooms. Where this happens in front of the same class of pupils, the support teacher may have a credibility problem. But at Whitmore School, teachers found that having two adults in classrooms had a calming effect.

(g) *The status of the support teacher in the eyes of the pupils.*

Children sometimes have strange notions about support teachers: they frequently ask if they are students. Support teachers have sometimes found it necessary to establish their authority in secondary classrooms. Their position in the eyes of pupils depends in part on their role in the lesson. Marginalization by the mainstream teacher may lead to marginalization by pupils. In Ron Best's School B, the Head of Supportive Education was variously described by pupils as 'a normal teacher', 'helping those who are not the more intelligent ones' and 'an odd-job teacher that does a bit of everything' (Best, 1987, p. 79).

(h) *The status of the support teacher in the eyes of mainstream teachers.*

Many support teachers have found that they need to do some class teaching to maintain their credentials with mainstream teachers. At the Grove School (Reader 2, Chapter 1), higher pay for support teachers fuelled complaints that they were not 'real' teachers. To maintain their credibility, support teachers took assemblies and played a full part in staff and curriculum meetings.

SUPPORT TEACHERS AS CHANGE AGENTS

3.16 The changes during the 1980s involved additional responsibilities for support teachers. They had been used to taking responsibility for a part of the education of some children. Now, with a growing acceptance among those in charge of learning support services that curricula had to be reformed, support teachers began to be seen as the people who would carry through this reform.

Activity 3 Spreading the gospel?

Now read 'A new role for a support service' by Linda Harland (Reader 1, Chapter 9).

In this chapter, Linda Harland examines the way in which three support teachers attempted to cope with their new-found responsibilities. You will find that she illustrates aspects of points (a) to (e) immediately above. You may find it useful to make notes under these headings. As you read this chapter think about these questions:

- Who has the power to make changes in the curriculum in a particular classroom?

- What skills and knowledge would a support teacher need in order to fulfil the role expected of them in the LEA that Linda Harland describes?

3.17 What does the experience of these three support teachers tell us about learning support as a means to reform the curriculum? First, policymakers in this LEA failed to take into account the experience and preferences of the support teachers. In 'A County' many of these teachers were experts in the teaching of reading in individual and small-group settings, yet they were suddenly expected to advise on many other aspects of the curriculum in mainstream classrooms. Second, the support teachers had to come to terms with the expectations of class teachers well used to a support service that worked with individual children. Third, the support teachers had to reckon with their temporary and relatively powerless status in the school. None of the class teachers was obliged to follow the support teachers' wishes. This placed the onus for negotiating a change on the support teachers. What these teachers were able to do in practice represented a compromise between the aims of the new policy, their own preferences and resources, and the circumstances in which they had to work.

IS SUPPORT TEACHING STILL AN 'AMBULANCE SERVICE'?

3.18   What exactly did 'A County' want from its support teachers? When the Inspector for Special Educational Needs said that the main objective of the Support Teams was to 'offer an appropriate level of support' what did he mean? Would the Inspector have approved of the work done by the three teachers? When the support teachers thought they would be responsible for adapting the National Curriculum to make it accessible for children with learning difficulties, what did they have in mind? In the next reading we shall explore two alternative approaches to support teaching in mainstream classes, aspects of which we can see in the work of Angela, Deidre and Sue.

Activity 4   Changing children, changing curricula

Now read 'Evaluating support teaching' by Susan Hart (Reader 1, Chapter 8).

Susan Hart makes a distinction between an 'individual' approach and a 'whole curriculum' approach to support teaching. As you read, concentrate on:

(a) the defining features of these two approaches;

(b) the arguments in favour of the whole curriculum approach.

You may find it useful to relate the arguments in this chapter back to the discussion in para. 3.15. You will find that Susan Hart makes points related to (a) and (b) in particular. Depending on your time and interest, it may also be useful to look at how the two approaches are manifested in the work of the three teachers described by Linda Harland, and in the accounts of Whitmore and the Grove School. If you are a support teacher, or if you work with one, you might wish to relate your own practice to the two approaches.

3.19   The essence of Susan Hart's argument against the individual approach is simple:

(a) It can isolate and stigmatize as much as withdrawal work did. In Section 6, I shall argue that an exclusive focus on individual work is not just socially isolating, but also denies children access to important learning resources.

(b) To be effective, the individual approach to support teaching requires certain conditions. Where these conditions are not present, support is not a worthwhile strategy. In order to create these conditions, the whole curriculum approach is needed. Once the right conditions are established, there is less need for support aimed at individuals.

3.20 But Susan Hart does not conclude that individual support is never appropriate. At Whitmore School learning support staff have worked at both levels. Reader 2, Chapter 2, Section 3 describes curricula in English and RE developed by pairs of class and support teachers. In Section 2 of the chapter there are several examples of individual support for spelling, writing, explaining a task, getting started, etc. The children with physical and sensory disabilities at The Grove School need considerable individual support to ensure their full participation in the curriculum, delivered by a team of support teachers and classroom assistants. In Unit 8/9 we shall look in more detail at some aspects of this support. You may find it useful to read Susan Hart's description of the individual approach again, thinking this time about the needs of children like Brendon and Madeleine at The Grove School. Is individual support all that is needed for these pupils?

3.21 Susan Hart is not concerned with the question of whether support teachers have the power, skills and knowledge to make fundamental changes in the curriculum. We have already seen three support teachers adjusting their work to their own abilities, interests and circumstances. Hart points out that there is nothing in the 'whole curriculum' approach which makes support teachers the only people who can do it. This begs some questions. Are they the best people to do it? Can the use of support teachers as agents of whole curriculum change be a self-destructive strategy? If a support teacher is committed to individual work on isolated basic literacy skills, is she the best person to ask to help other teachers to find alternatives to this approach? Could the interests of whole curriculum reform be better served without such an intervention?

3.22 We have now reached a stage in the argument where we need to look closer at the content and structure of the mainstream curriculum in order to understand the sources of learning difficulties that children may face, and to see in practical terms what the opportunities for change are.

SUMMARY

3.23 In-class support was developed as an important strategy for helping children who experience difficulties in mainstream lessons. There were several reasons. They concerned giving all the children access to a broad and coherent curriculum, making sure that as many children as possible benefited from the services of learning support teachers, reforming the curriculum that was causing the problems, avoiding stigma, and giving all teachers a sense of responsibility for all children.

3.24 The move to in-class support does not mean that small-group and individual teaching is universally inappropriate. Some schools use both in-class support and withdrawal as parts of an overall learning support strategy.

3.25 The value of in-class support is affected by many factors: the quality of planning, both teachers' styles, methods and views of learning support, the support teacher's knowledge of the subject matter, the personal and professional relationship between the two teachers, and their relationships with pupils.

3.26 In some schools support teachers have been expected to help mainstream teachers to change their teaching methods. How far they can do this depends on their personal skills and preferences, and the teachers and schools with whom they have to work.

3.27 Although one aim of in-class support has been to reform the mainstream curriculum, it has not always achieved this goal. Sometimes it has just involved a change of place in which individual child-focused activities are carried out, leaving unaffected the problems that in-class support was meant to tackle.

4 COPING WITH CLASSROOM TEXTS

POLONIUS: What do you read, my lord?

HAMLET: Words, words, words

(*Hamlet*, Act 2, Scene 2)

4.1 Many, probably most, lessons rely on children's ability to extract meaning from texts of one kind or another: worksheets, picture books, textbooks, dictionaries, pamphlets, documents, recipe cards, timetables, maps, diagrams, manuals, databases, black/white-board instructions, forms, music, photographs, newspapers, magazines, letters, and so on. Some of these consist only of words, some contain only non-verbal, visual information, and others combine the two. Some of them convey instructions to pupils and provide formats for recording, others convey substantive information, and some do both. I am going to refer to all these things as 'texts', whether they contain words, pictures or a mixture of the two. All of them are potential sources of difficulty for children; problems in using texts are among the commonest reasons why children are said to have learning difficulties.

4.2 Written language poses difficulties for children over and above those they face with spoken language for a number of reasons. In the first place, it uses structures that are unfamiliar in spoken language, so children have not only to learn how the letters and words represent sounds, but they also have to learn new forms of language. Second, written language is not generally supported by contextual information. For example, if someone belches and then says 'please excuse my flatulence', even if you have not heard this word before, you can make a reasonable guess at what it means. But in written language, we are much more dependent on the information carried by the words themselves. Third, in spoken language, intonation, stress and pausing, known collectively as 'prosody', are important ways of conveying meaning, as you will discover immediately if you ask someone to read a few sentences in a monotone, and without varying the pauses between the words. Punctuation in written language does some of the work of prosody, but it is not a complete substitute. In this section I am going to look at how learning difficulties can arise if we fail to recognize what is involved in reading a text, and how such learning difficulties might be alleviated.

HOW A TEXT CAN BE DIFFICULT

4.3   As skilled adult readers it can be very hard to see the problems that texts generate for children, because we are usually unaware of the strategies we use to understand them. It is tempting to think that the only difficulties children might have are to do with linking the graphic images on the page to the sounds of spoken language. To get some idea of the many ways in which a text can be difficult to understand, I shall begin by looking at one example in some detail. This is a text that I encountered in a Year 6, inner-city classroom. The class contained children described by their teacher as having learning difficulties. The lesson was about Morse code. The children had been given a number of tasks to complete. These included writing a message in Morse code and writing 'four fascinating facts about Samuel Morse'. To do the second of these tasks, the class had a number of copies of an account of Samuel Morse's life, of which the following is an excerpt:

> MORSE, Samuel Finley Breese (1791–1872). The inventor of the electromagnetic telegraph and of the Morse code used for telegraphic messages was an American artist named Samuel Morse. He was born at Charlestown, Massachusetts, the son of Jedidiah Morse, a Congregationalist minister and geographer. Samuel attended Yale College, where he became a painter, and went to London to study.
>
> In 1832, on his return from a second visit to Europe, Morse gave up painting and set to work to invent the telegraph. For years he had little money and made his own models and parts. At last in 1837 he was able to exhibit a working telegraph instrument in New York. For some time no government would take an interest in the invention but in 1844 a telegraph line was set up between Baltimore and Washington (about 60 kilometres, or 37 miles). Later, Morse became interested in the first attempts to lay a telegraph cable across the Atlantic.
>
> Morse's invention was based on the discovery made in 1820 by the Dane, H. C. Oersted, that a magnetic needle pivoted so as to swing freely was deflected, or twisted, when a wire carrying an electric current was brought near it. Morse made an instrument in which an electric current, when turned on, worked an electromagnet which

caused a pencil to mark a moving strip of paper. The electric current was supplied from a battery and was turned on and off by means of a simple tapping 'key'.

(*Children's Encyclopaedia Britannica*, 1989, Vol. 12, pp. 114–15)

Activity 5   A comprehension exercise

What are the difficulties that a child might face in understanding this text? I would like you to suppose for this exercise that sounding out the individual words on the page is not a problem. What is there in the structure and content of this extract that might make it difficult to understand? Note down the points that occur to you. This is a good exercise to do in a group.

4.4   This was not an easy text for the children in this class to understand for many reasons, which I shall discuss under five headings.

Vocabulary

4.5 The extract is full of technical and uncommon terms: 'electromagnetic telegraph', 'Congregationalist', 'Dane', 'pivoted', 'deflected'. There are also more common words that are used in special senses, or whose precise meaning must be inferred from the rest of the text. The tapping 'key' is not a key of the kind that opens doors. The 'models' that Morse made are not toys, and he did not make them just for fun. Building models is part of the design process. But the text leaves the reader to infer this. And what about 'painter'? Is that a painter and decorator, or an artist?

Sentence structure

4.6 Many sentences in the extract are long and complex. They compress large amounts of information. Take the first sentence: 'The inventor of the electromagnetic telegraph and of the Morse code used for telegraphic messages was an American artist named Samuel Morse'. This does the work of five separate propositions:

- Samuel Morse invented Morse code.
- Samuel Morse invented the electromagnetic telegraph.
- Morse code is used for telegraphic messages.
- Samuel Morse was American.
- Samuel Morse was an artist.

4.7 The author manages to say all this in one sentence by giving each part of the sentence a complex structure of its own. There are fifteen words before we get to the main verb, 'was'. To understand this first part of the sentence, the reader must hold on to the idea that there is an inventor whilst reading what it was that was invented, before finding out who the inventor was. This poses quite a strain on memory. Whilst finding out what was invented, the reader has to cope with the first verb in the sentence, 'used'. She has to understand that this verb, and the three words that follow it, tell her about Morse code, not about the inventor; the sentence does not read 'The inventor used for telegraphic messages was an American artist'. Once past the main verb 'was', the reader then has to realize that the next six words belong together. The sentence is potentially complete after 'American'. But then what does the reader do with 'artist named Samuel Morse'?

4.8 The sentence manages to compress so much information by using a number of grammatical devices. One is the subordinate clause, such as 'used for telegraphic messages' and 'named Samuel Morse'. Another is the extensive elaboration of the main elements of the sentence. Rather than 'the inventor of Morse code', we have the full fifteen word subject of the sentence. In this sentence are to be found four 'fascinating facts' about Samuel Morse, but considerable work is needed to prise them out. This is not the most complex sentence in the extract. You might try a similar analysis of the sentence beginning 'Morse's invention' in the third paragraph.

Discourse structure

4.9   In various ways this extract 'hangs together'. Linguists refer to this characteristic of texts as its discourse structure. There is both a global and local structure. The global structure of a text refers to its overall organization. It affects the ease with which readers can recall and understand the text. In the extract, the first paragraph introduces Samuel Morse as the main protagonist. The second paragraph tells us about how he came to invent the telegraph, and the third paragraph tells us about the invention itself. But this global structure is not signalled explicitly. The reader who can understand each paragraph will more easily discern it, and in the process will make more sense of the text as a whole. The reader who can make no sense of any of the parts will not be able to see how they relate to the whole.

4.10   Local discourse structure refers to the ways in which the sentences of a text are linked together. Texts that appear to be a string of unconnected sentences are difficult to follow, so the many ways in which sentences are tied together are themselves ways to reduce reading difficulty. But these devices can also be the source of problems. One device used to link the sentences of this extract together is the repetition of certain words – 'Morse', 'telegraph', and 'invention', for example. In most cases repetition helps understanding. A second device is the use of pronouns as substitutes for the words they refer to. An example is 'he' in the sentence in the second paragraph that begins 'For years'. This 'he' means Samuel Morse – a link that the reader must deduce for herself. A third device is the use of synonyms. An example is 'Morse's invention' at the start of the third paragraph. This refers to the telegraph, not to Morse code or anything else, though the text does not make this explicit. A fourth device is ellipsis. An example is 'but decided to become a painter'. Here the subject of the sentence is left out – elided – altogether. The reader must infer that it is Morse who did the deciding. To understand the text, the reader has to cope with all these devices.

World knowledge

4.11   Suppose that you have never heard of Massachusetts. Is it a thing, a person, a place? If it is a person, he might be the son of Jedidiah Morse. If it is a place it might be part of the name of the place where Morse was born. Knowing about 'Massachusetts' helps the reader to understand the sentence it is part of. Linguists distinguish between 'linguistic knowledge' – knowledge of the organization of language – and the 'world knowledge' needed to understand a text. Knowing about Massachusetts is only a minor example of the world knowledge needed to understand this text fully. The reader also needs to know a lot about what telegraphs are and how they work. What do they do? What are they for? Why do they have 'lines' and 'cables'? What have magnetism and electricity got to do with them? Why should governments be interested in telegraphs? Without answers to these questions the meaning of the text will remain obscure, even if the reader can understand the individual words, sentence and discourse structures.

How the text is used

4.12   To me, some of the meaning is obscure, since my knowledge of telegraphy is very rudimentary, but that does not matter too much, because I can make judgements about which parts of the texts are important and which are not. I rate the fact that Morse invented the telegraph as more important than his father's job. But sifting from a text the items of information that matter depends on having a clear purpose in reading it. In the lesson where this extract was used, the children's purpose was to find 'four fascinating facts' about Morse. We need to imagine what expectations this might set up in children's minds. Somewhere in the text are to be found the four fascinating facts. Perhaps not all the facts are fascinating, but unfortunately there is no hint as to which ones are the magic four, and there is no other obvious way to sort out the facts that are fascinating from the rest. So getting meaning from a text depends on having a purpose in reading it which the text can satisfy.

4.13   Using this example, I have described four sources of potential difficulty in a text: vocabulary, sentence structure, discourse structure and the world knowledge it assumes. And I have argued that the difficulty of a text also depends on how it is used. Now I am going to use these ideas to examine and evaluate one of the best known approaches to assessing the difficulty of a text: the use of readability formulae.

READABILITY FORMULAE

4.14   Readability formulae are measurements which give a 'reading level' for a text, usually expressed as the reading age for which the text would be appropriate. There are a number of alternative formulae, the uses and drawbacks of which are thoroughly discussed by Harrison (1980). Nearly all of them are based on two aspects of a text: the number of words in sentences and the length of the words, usually measured in syllables. The formulae depend on two ideas: long sentences are harder to read than short sentences; and long words are harder to read than short words. Generally speaking, the longer the sentences and the more polysyllabic words in a text, the higher its readability level. One commonly used formula is the Flesch formula, which Harrison recommends for secondary level. This produces a score based on the number of syllables in a 100-word passage, and the average number of words per sentence. The score can then be converted into a reading age level. A formula useful at primary level, based on the same two variables is the Powers–Sumner–Kearl formula. In the Appendix, I have described how these two formulae work.

4.15   Readability formulae are usually used to gain a quick impression of the difficulty of a book, and can be a useful first stage in reviewing material. But they can be misleading as well. First of all, they are not always reliable. Texts can vary a great deal from page to page in their readability level, so the measured readability of the text can depend on which sample is analysed (Stokes, 1978). Secondly, they capture only some of the factors that can make a text difficult to read. Readability formulae concentrate on indirect assessments of sentence structure and vocabulary, measured by sentence length and word length. They do not help to assess the problems created by the discourse structure or the subject matter of a text. So a low readability level does not guarantee that the text will be easily understood; indeed, if we rely too much on simplifying texts by reducing sentence and word length, the result can sometimes be texts that are harder to understand as a result of a discourse structure that is more difficult to cope with, or assumptions about the reader's world knowledge that remain unchallenged.

DISCOURSE STRUCTURE

4.16   One effect of applying readability formulae in an undiscriminating manner is the production of texts which consist of strings of short unconnected sentences. Katherine Perera (1984), who provides a detailed analysis of the difficulties generated by both sentence and discourse structure, warns against this tendency, as illustrated in this example from a book aimed at 6- to 8-year-olds:

> **Grizzly Bears**
>
> Huge brown bears living in North America are called Grizzlies.
>
> Once they were thought to belong to a separate species. Now they are quite rare.
>
> Grizzlies used to prey upon the herds of bison. When the bison became scarce the Grizzlies became fewer too.
>
> In some places the forests where they lived have been cut down.
>
> (Quoted in Perera, 1984, p. 323)

4.17   Perera argues that the nature of the connections between the six sentences in this text may create difficulties for the reader. 'Once' and 'now' at the start of the second and third sentences imply a contrast between the two, but in fact there is none, so the expectation created in the second sentence leads nowhere. The last three sentences explain why grizzlies are now rare, but there is nothing to help the reader to connect sentences 4 to 6 to the third sentence. Longer sentences, which made the links between the ideas explicit, might improve the text.

4.18   A discourse structure that is familiar and easy to understand is an important aid for children who are in the early stages of learning to read.

Most of the books that children learn to read with at school are stories of one kind or another. Stories have a predictable, coherent structure that most children become familiar with well before they come to school, through stories told and read to them by family and friends. They contain elements such as settings and characters integrated into a plot made up of connected episodes. Children's understanding of narrative has become an important part of research into the development of reading; there is increasing evidence that the narrative skills of preschool children are related to their later literacy development (Snow, 1983; Wells, 1985).

4.19 Children's knowledge of narrative structure is an important resource that they can bring to the task of making sense of school texts. But it is not always possible to use this resource, since some texts that purport to be narratives lack a coherent and cohesive discourse structure which children can use to impose order on the text. Such texts may be more difficult to read as a result. This is well illustrated in an analysis by Barrie Wade (1990) of an extract from a reading scheme:

> Consider this three-page extract from a popular reading scheme:
>
> 1   Come on, Pat.
> 2   Come and play in the boat, Jane.
> 3   Come on, he says.
> 4   Look at me in the boat.
> 5   Look at me, Jane.
> 6   Look at me, says Peter.
> 7   Get in the boat, Jane.
> 8   The fish can see you in the water.
> 9   Get in the boat, says Peter.
> 10 Peter can see a fish in the water.
> 11 They want to fish.
> 12 Jane is in the water and Peter is in the boat.
> 13 Jump up. Jump up here.
> 14 Come and play on the boat.
> 15 Come on the boat.
> 16 Come on, says Peter.
> 17 They like to play on the boat.
> 18 Jane and Peter play in the water.
>
> … What meanings can be constructed from the cohesion and coherence of this episode? The scene is fairly clear. Peter (the boy) is

engaged in activity and the passage, as well as narrating what happens, contains frequent exhortations to Jane (the girl) and to Pat (the dog), who are somewhat more passive, to get into the action. There are frequent exhortations to 'look', to 'come', to 'jump up' and to 'get in', both before and after the explicit and descriptive stage (12):

> Jane is in the water and Peter is in the boat.

The causal links seem to be straightforward. Peter wants Jane to play with him in the boat (2) *because* they like to play in the boat (17). Within this framework other causal connections may be perceived, for example between 7 and 8: Jane is invited to get in the boat *because* the fish can see her while she remains out of it. This kind of connection seems reasonable since 11 tells us 'they want to fish'. (Presumably they will have more chance of catching a fish if it cannot see them.)

We have begun – as a child would need to – to make sense of a passage such as this. We have focused upon the setting in which the characters are placed and we have begun to make connections between the various stages of the events and episodes. However, as Macbeth once said when he was analysing the causal connections of a projected episode, 'We will proceed no further in this business'. Our sequence of numbered story stages 1–18, I must now reveal, is not as it appears in the original text. The elements do, in fact, come in order, *but the order is exactly reversed in the original book.*

Having reread the passage in its proper order, starting at 18 and finishing at 1, a reader will have established a similarly coherent picture to the one we have already discussed. This passage makes nearly as much sense when we read back to front as when read in the intended order. We could speculate whether other arrangements of the 18 elements, even a random ordering, would make as much sense. Is such arbitrariness helpful to children who have reached the third book in their scheme? I would argue that at this time it is preferable, even essential, to use material where links, connections and relationships reinforce the patterns that a child has already learned exist in language and communication. It seems that some children have difficulty simply because the language of such readers appears arbitrary.
(Wade, 1990, pp. 21–4)

4.20 So far we have been concerned with the discourse structure of continuous prose. Many of the materials that children face in classrooms are not of this form. Worksheets, maths scheme books, exercises from textbooks also have what we can look on as discourse structures – ways in which the parts are related to each other and to the whole. As with continuous texts, the structure of non-prose texts can create, as well as avoid, difficulties for the pupils who have to use them.

Activity 6 How do worksheets work?

Figure 2 shows an example of a typical primary maths exercise. This is one of the worksheets used in the Key Stage 1 Standard Assessment Tasks in 1991, designed to assess performance in multiplication and division at Level 3 of the National Curriculum in mathematics. (If you are not familiar with National Curriculum terminology, don't worry. Unit 8/9 explains it.) Teachers were instructed to 'ask the children to work out the cost of the items and write down the answers in the space provided' and to 'make sure children understand what they have to do before they start'. The sheet consists of elements – texts, numbers, lines and drawings – which stand in various relationships to each other. These relationships constitute the discourse structure of the sheet. Note down the elements of the discourse structure of this sheet that you can identify. My version follows.

4.21 I have found the following features of the organization of this sheet. You may have found others.

(a) There are short horizontal lines. These are immediately below the space where the answer to the problem on the left of the line is to be written. This is an example of a *spatial* convention, in that the conceptual relationship between two parts of the text are signalled by their spatial relationship to each other.

(b) The numbers in rectangles connected by lines to the food in the lower two boxes on the page are price tags. They tell the reader how much one (and no other number) of these items costs. This is another spatial convention. It also involves a convention, derived from world knowledge, that numbers on labels attached to food are price tags.

(c) In the top half of the sheet, phrases are paired together, so that, for example, '1 loaf of bread' belongs with '3 loaves of bread'. This is helped by the repetition of words, a device I identified earlier. This is one of many types of *linguistic* convention.

(d) Another linguistic convention is involved in '3 loaves of bread'. This is an elliptical form of 'What is the price of 3 loaves of bread?'.

(e) The drawings are linked to the phrases and sentences below them. This is done in various ways. There are spatial links, although the spatial information is rather ambiguous in some cases, like the small cake. There is a linguistic link in the case of the crisps, and there are what we can call *iconic* links, associating the picture of the roll, for example, with the sentence below it.

(f) There is a link between each pair of items of food. In answering a problem such as '3 loaves of bread', children must accept that they can get the price of one of these loaves from the item above it, and that all the loaves are at this price. Now this assumption is a rather special feature of this text: out in the world, loaves of bread are not all the same price; in the little world created by this sheet, they are.

Figure 2   Maths worksheet from the 1991 Standard Assessment Tasks
(© HMSO)

We might call this a *school knowledge* discourse convention. In Section 5, I shall be discussing the place of such conventions in lessons in more detail, where we shall see how the clash between school knowledge conventions and children's world knowledge can cause difficulties.

(g) Print size and style are used to indicate categories of information. Thus the phrases identifying the items of food are all in plain text of one size; the answers in the top half of the sheet are in a larger bold typeface; the four 'price tags' are in bold typeface the same size as the items of food. We can refer to these as *print* conventions.

4.22   If the reader fails to understand some of the conventions I have described then the task may not be successfully completed. Misunderstanding of the discourse structure of this sheet would be undesirable, since this task is not a test of worksheet reading, but of multiplication and division. Some children will have no problem in understanding its structure, having had extensive experience of the conventions it uses. Others may depend heavily on their teacher's explanation. I have chosen this example to show how even the most basic and carefully planned non-prose text uses spatial, iconic, linguistic, print and school knowledge conventions, which are not explicitly declared, to carry meaning. Just like the discourse conventions I discussed earlier in looking at prose texts, these conventions can be powerful devices to clarify meaning. The layout of the maths sheet helps a great deal by separating the four sets of items. It might have been even better if each item had been separately boxed off.

4.23   Learning difficulties resulting from misreading or not understanding discourse conventions in worksheets are a common classroom experience. Robert Hull (1985) provides an example from a Year 7 English lesson in which five pupils had been given a special task because they found the work the others were doing too difficult. They had to complete the exercise from a comprehension book, shown in Figure 3. Hull notes that one pupil, who was also receiving remedial support in withdrawal lessons, was unable to begin this task at all.

Activity 7   More than just a worksheet

What implicit discourse conventions does this text use? What does the reader have to know about its discourse structure in order to complete the exercise? Hull's analysis follows.

Though they are not necessarily available to the pupil, a number of assumptions are made by the writer about how the page will be read. The words in the box are used to complete the sentences. They need to be combined to do so ('keeps … cool'). The pictures describe sentences; so, they are clues. The order of the pictures is the order of the sentences; so, the pictures have to be read down the left then down the right. One could also quibble and say 'finish the sentence' refers to phrases such as 'The whole hat'. And a natural ending 'keeps the sun off' is not offered. The obscurity of the pictures' meanings is such that the text is necessary to interpret them; pupils need the answer to understand the clue.

(Hull, 1985, p. 97)

A man named Stetson made a special kind of felt hat for cowboys. That is why cowboys' hats are often called Stetsons.

The pictures show you some of the many uses of a Stetson hat. Write about them by finishing the sentences.

campfire	head
cool	horse
drinking	keeps
ears	pillow
eyes	pulled
fan	tied
water	

A cowboy's hat is often called a Stetson.

The air inside the high crown ....

The wide brim keeps the sun ....

On rainy days ....

In cold weather ....

The brim can also ....

The whole hat ....

He can use it ....

Rolled up it ....

Figure 3   More than just a hat (Hull, 1985, p. 97)

4.24 Now this example is particularly significant: it was a task set for a child who was experiencing difficulties on the assumption that it was easier than the work for the rest of the class. If you are a teacher, you may find it useful to look at a selection of worksheets and other non-prose materials used in your school, especially those used with children with learning difficulties, in terms of the conventions they use to convey their meaning and the difficulties that they may create. In the last part of this section I shall briefly explore ways in which we might try to overcome some of the difficulties created by texts.

SOLUTIONS

Simplifying texts

4.25 Learning support teachers, especially at secondary level, often spend a lot of time working with colleagues to review and simplify learning texts to make them easier to understand. Helen Currie (1990), a special needs support teacher, describes how she worked with subject teachers from three comprehensive schools on science and humanities material using five simple rules:

(a) shorten long sentences;

(b) replace unusual words with more common ones;

(c) replace metaphorical phrases with more literal ones;

(d) clarify the purpose of digressions;

(e) improve legibility.

These rules were followed to rewrite texts used with Key Stage 3 mixed-ability classes. The aim was not to produce alternative versions of texts for poor readers but to make the texts more accessible to all pupils.

4.26 Rule (e) was applied in different ways in each school. In one school, it meant:

1 double spacing between statements, questions, etc.;

2 treble spacing between sections;

3 larger print;

4 clearer labelling and improved positioning of diagrams and charts in relation to text;

5 boxing of important information and instructions;

6 underlining of keywords.

Guidelines 1, 2, 4 and 5 involve spatial conventions which help to signal the structural components of the text: what words and diagrams 'go together'. Guidelines 5 and 6 use print conventions to indicate which parts of the text are more important than others. These six rules only hint at the possible variations that can make a difference to the legibility of a text. According to Harrison (1980) over 2000 variables have been identified: word spacing, line length, line breaks, upper or lower case, the particular typeface used, and many more. Most of these make only the most marginal difference to understanding the text. They are thoroughly reviewed in Watts and Nisbet (1974).

Activity 8 Rewriting a worksheet

Figure 4 shows one of the worksheets that was rewritten as a result of Helen Currie and her colleagues' work. Read both versions, note the differences and assess whether you think the revised version is an improvement on the original.

4.27 I noted the following changes:

(a) Instructions are put into a chronological sequence (but notice that this breaks down with instructions 7 and 8). This sequencing has the advantage of allowing the reader to work through the text

Original version

Experiment 2 - At what temperature does water boil?

Put about 50ml of water into a large beaker. You will also need a tripod, gauze, bunsen burner, stop clock and thermometer.

Draw out a table like the one below - remember that you don't yet know how big the table will be.

Time in minutes	Temperature in °C
start	
2	
4	
6	
8	
10	
12	
14	

1. Find out the temperature of the cold water. This is your start temperature so put it in your table.

2. Light your bunsen and make sure that the air-hole is half open.
   As soon as you put the bunsen under your beaker, START the clock.

3. Take the temperature on the thermometer every two minutes, but DO NOT STOP THE CLOCK.

What is the highest temperature the thermometer reads?

This is called the boiling point of water.

COPY

   The boiling point of water is ...... °C

Revised version

Experiment 2

At what temperature does water boil?

First get these things -
   large beaker
   tripod
   gauze
   bunsen burner
   stop clock
   thermometer.

1. Put about 50 ml of water into the large beaker.

2. Draw this table into your book. You will not know how big the table will be so leave some space at the bottom.

Time in minutes	Temperature in °C
start	
2	
4	
6	
8	
10	
12	
14	

3. Find out the temperature of the cold water. This is your start temperature.

4. Write your start temperature on your table in your book.

5. Light your bunsen and make sure that the air hole is half open.

6. Put the bunsen under your beaker and start the clock straight away.

7. Every two minutes read the temperature on the thermometer but do not stop the clock.

8. Write down the temperature on the table in your book.

9. Notice the highest temperature the thermometer reads.

This is called the boiling point of water.

10. COPY

   The boiling point of water is ...... °C

Figure 4   Science worksheet

systematically, pausing after each instruction to do what it says. It means that children do not have to read the whole sheet first. On the other hand, reading the whole text explains the purpose of the experiment, and seeing the purpose of an activity is crucial to successful participation in it – a point I shall take up later on.

(b) All the instructions except the first are numbered and laid out in the same way, helping the reader to see that they are text elements of the same kind.

(c) Instructions are made more explicit: for example, the potentially troublesome 'as soon as' is removed so that it is clear that putting the bunsen under the beaker refers to an instruction. In the revised version, the reader is told to read the temperature and then write it down. However, the penalty for this is that there is no longer a clear link between the revised instructions 7 and 8. The reader has to deduce that the temperature must be written down each and every time it is read.

(d) Key actions are underlined in the revised version throughout the sheet. Whether these are actually the most important words to highlight depends on the use of the sheet in practice. I didn't find the use of underlining *excessive*, but OVERUSE of *different type styles* can sometimes make a text more DIFFICULT to use.

4.28 The result of simplifying this and other texts is that they became longer, but took less time for classes to work through. But there is a danger that attempts to simplify can also lead to texts being less explicit and so more difficult to understand, if the focus is exclusively on reducing the amount and grammatical complexity of the language in the text. A history teacher observed by Robert Hull was concerned that the textbook she was using with Year 7 groups was too difficult. She had been using it to teach about the problems that Queen Elizabeth I faced on her accession. In an attempt to make the ideas more accessible, she used the sheet shown in Figure 5, in which the text is condensed into main points, shown metaphorically as boulders blocking Elizabeth's path. This removes most of the language which children were finding difficult, but it does not thereby make the ideas any more comprehensible. Indeed, by stripping away detail, Elizabeth's problems became more abstract; the description moves further from the concrete reality of the politics and economy of the time. What, for example, might 'shortage of money' mean? The visual metaphor itself was not understood as such by all the pupils: some of them thought that the path was a real one they could have walked on.

4.29 Simplification needs to be seen through the learner's eyes. The compression of information in this history sheet does not simplify the problem for the learner at all. 'Simplification' from the learner's perspective may involve a text which appears on the surface to be more complex. Some writers, such as Katherine Perera (1984), have argued that

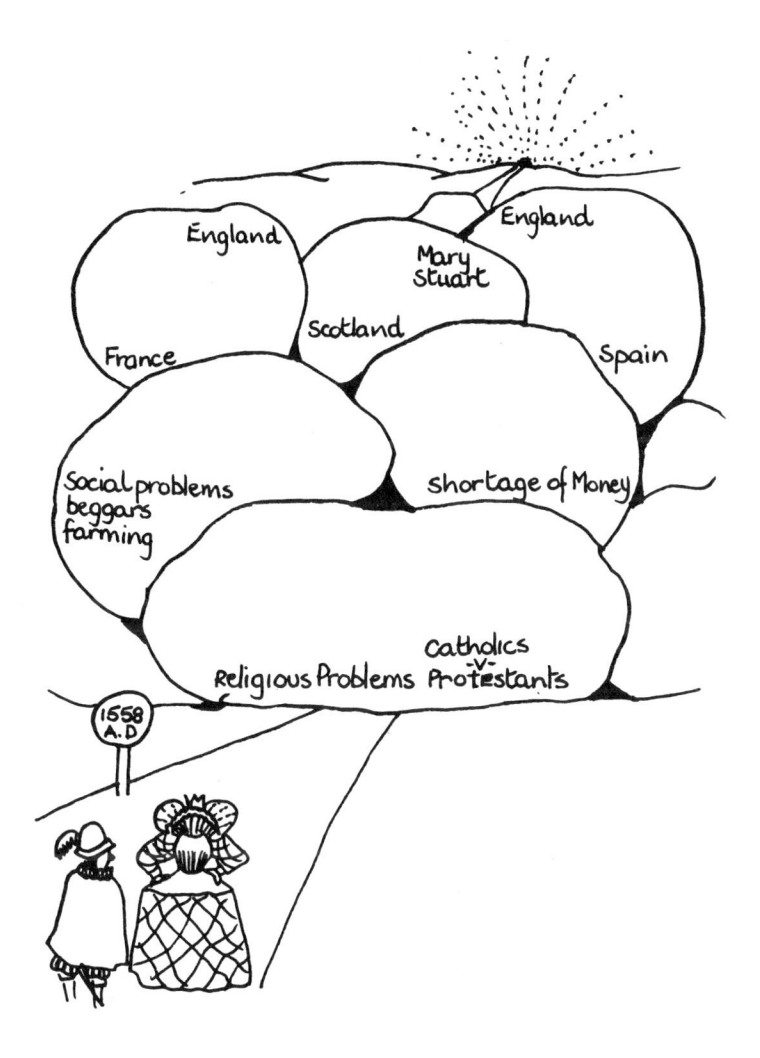

Some Obstacles in the Path of Elizabeth I

Figure 5 'Simplified' history worksheet (Hull, 1985, p. 72)

we can make non-fiction more accessible by presenting it in a narrative style, exploiting children's knowledge of and commitment to stories. But there are dangers here, for stories can be badly or well done, as Robert Hull points out:

> 'Informative' but inadequate narrative is so widespread that examples can be found almost at random. This is the first paragraph of *Columbus and the Age of Exploration*, by Stewart Ross, published by Wayland in 1985:
>
> > In the crow's nest the look-out screwed his eyes up against the glare of the tropical sun. Beneath him the little forty-ton ship Nina rolled heavily in the Arctic swell. The sailor took a piece

> of dry biscuit from his pocket. It tasted foul, but there was no other food. They had been at sea for forty days now and supplies were getting perilously low.

The problem here is the writer's reluctance to commit himself to narrative, and to the viewpoint of his narrator. He has half an eye on the fiction and one-and-a-half on the information; the look-out screws up his eyes to think about the food situation and the weight of the boat. There's no focus; we can't believe it as narrative ...

Perhaps, some might say, you can only do it in some subjects. With maths, chemistry and physics, especially, text has to be impersonal, objective, etc. This is surely nonsense. Here is some physics:

> Go with some friends under the hatches of some big ship and see that you have some small birds with you, and also a small bucket with a hole in suspended high above another one, so that the water will drip slowly from the higher to the lower one. Observe very carefully, when the boat is standing still, the way the birds dart about to and fro in all directions, and the drops fall into the bucket underneath. Get the ship to move as fast as it can and so long as the movement is steady and uniform, you will not see the slightest alteration in the way the birds fly or water falls, and you will not be able to tell from them whether the ship is moving or not.

Physics to *read* ... from Galileo.
(Hull, 1990, pp. 17, 19)

Working actively with texts

4.30 Although I have stressed the way in which undeclared textual conventions can create problems for children, there is no escape from them, and indeed it is the responsibility of teachers to help children to develop an understanding of them. One way to make a prose text clearer is for a skilled reader to read it aloud. The addition of intonation and pausing can help greatly to clarify meaning. The skilled reader does not have to be a teacher. In a classroom in which it is the norm for pupils to work together in mixed groups, less confident readers have many opportunities to learn about how to read a text from their peers. Another way is to add extra devices to the text, such as highlighting and underlining, or providing keywords on separate cards to draw attention to the more important elements.

4.31 Equally important are opportunities to work on and talk about the ways in which texts are constructed. These need not just be teacher explanations of texts, but active work by pupils on texts. Directed Activities Related to Text (DARTs), developed in the Schools Council Effective Use of Reading Project (Lunzer and Gardner, 1979; Lunzer, Gardner, Davies and Greene, 1984), illustrate a number of methods for use in small-group work, such as underlining, labelling main ideas, drawing diagrams to represent the structure of the text, tabulating information, splitting the text into segments, debating what should go in places where text has been deleted, completing stories, predicting what would be in a text from its title. In encouraging you to work closely with texts in the course material, we hope that you will engage in the same kind of process. Unit 10 will be a series of Directed Activities Related to Text, as are many of the activities in the course as a whole.

4.32 Children can also learn much about how texts are structured by creating them for themselves. In doing so, they have to work actively with the conventions of text: they are encouraged by the nature of the task to reveal what they know about how texts are put together, and their work provides a meaningful context in which they and their teacher can talk about how texts are constructed. Thus writing is directly tied to developing an understanding of text structures and conventions. In TV4, you will see some pupils who have been identified as having learning difficulties developing a non-fiction, non-prose text for younger children. I shall discuss this episode in more detail in Section 6. Valerie Cherrington (1990) and Barrie Wade (1985) give useful examples of how groups of primary children have developed non-narrative texts for themselves and others. Cherrington describes work with a group of four Year 4 and 5 girls, one of whom was considered by their teacher to be 'lazy and underachieving', and another to be 'the least able' in the class. They produced a book on cruelty to animals, aimed at children of their own age. Having a clear purpose and audience for their work gave them the motivation to make sense of difficult texts:

> Texts were tackled in various ways. For example, the teacher read the text aloud ... and then discussed it with the children. This strategy allowed for exploration and consideration of such things as:
>
> - main headings and subheadings;
>
> - main ideas, supporting details;
>
> - interpreting dense and complex language, enabling children to discuss the information and then be in a better position to ask questions, answer questions and write in their own words.
>
> Some words had to be explained and discussed, for example, 'signals', 'respond', 'aggression'.
>
> It was important for the children to make sense of the information by relating it to experiences in their own lives ... During the supported reading sessions the teacher would sometimes ask the children to express the ideas in simpler language – as a rehearsal for writing for their intended audience.
>
> (Cherrington, 1990, pp. 142–3)

4.33 When the group began to turn the information into their own text, they had to work actively on how a text is built up through ideas that are linked together in a coherent discourse structure. You may recall

Christine Gilbert and Michael Hart's account of a similar approach used in religious education at Whitmore School (Reader 2, Chapter 2) in which pupils made booklets on major religions.

Diversifying texts

4.34 In simplifying a text, or supporting children's use of it with oral explanations, we make an intervention which alters some features of the lesson, but preserves others. In the case of the lesson on Morse code, we might rewrite the text to make it easier to help children to extract 'fascinating facts', but is the aim of the exercise to make this text more accessible, or to make the ideas of telegraphy and remote-coded communication more accessible? If it is the latter, then revising the text may not achieve much. During this lesson, I spoke to some of the children about the ideas behind the text. I asked them what Morse code was for, and why it mattered. Several believed it was designed to send secret messages. They had little notion about the conditions of communication under which it was invented: the absence of telephones and fast roads. I asked one pupil, identified as having learning difficulties, when Morse lived. She didn't know, and was astonished to learn that he was born 200 years ago. The problems with this text were profound. The 'world knowledge' that the text relied on for its sense was not available to many children in this class; simplification would do nothing to rectify this.

4.35 In the history worksheet in Figure 5 we have seen another example in which 'simplification' of a text has left its connection to the real events it refers to quite obscure. In accounting for what children learn in these circumstances, Robert Hull draws on a distinction made by philosophers between empirical and logical propositions. An empirical proposition is one that can in principle be verified, or falsified, by reference to the real world. An example is 'Morse code was first transmitted by telegraph wire'. Either it was or was not, and we can check this by looking at the evidence. A logical proposition is one whose truth depends on the conventions and rules of usage of its terms. For example, if I say that 'all gannols are fassid' and 'Pewig is a gannol', you will know that Pewig is fassid. You have no real world referents for these terms: the truth of the conclusion depends on the initial premises and the conventions of language use. Hull argues that much of the knowledge conveyed in school is seen by teachers as empirical, but learned by pupils as if it were logical, because they do not have adequate 'empirical moorings' for the words. Even if the Morse code text had been simplified so that the 'fascinating facts' could be extracted, to many of the children these 'facts' would not mean anything. It is more difficult to learn and remember meaningless material than to learn meaningful material – so when a text forces children to learn things which to them have no grounding in the real world, learning difficulties are created.

4.36 Some of these difficulties may be overcome if information and evidence from a variety of sources is used to replace and supplement texts, in order to give the ideas some 'empirical moorings'. Children learning about Morse code could look at and operate a telegraph device, or an electromagnet. Evidence from the period when Morse code was invented, in the form of diaries, posters and drawings could be used. Videos about what Morse code was for, and how it was used for military and civil purposes, might be available. As well as reducing children's dependence on text, having a diversity of resources gives children opportunities to select those resources that make sense to them.

4.37 Children can also provide some of the resources through their own activity. If we want them to understand the problems of remote communication, we can challenge groups to send messages from one side of the playground to the other without speech or writing. Ideas and solutions from different groups can be displayed and compared. Which of them might work over greater distances? What happens when you lose a visual link? To understand how Morse code works, children can make their own electromagnets and telegraphs (in the process learning some science) and then use them to transmit messages from one room to another. By doing so, the children engage actively in the lesson topic, and this helps them to attach meaning to the ideas. This active involvement of pupils also means that children have more opportunities to work at the ideas at their own level, and to relate what they already know to what they are learning. In Sections 5 and 6, I shall be looking further at the significance of active involvement in learning, especially for pupils described as having learning difficulties. But first, in the next section, I turn to the learning difficulties that can be created by the way spoken, as opposed to written forms of language, are used in classrooms.

SUMMARY

4.38 Children may experience difficulties in reading a prose text for several reasons to do with the way the text has been written. These include its vocabulary, sentence structure, global and local discourse structure, and the world knowledge it assumes in the reader. Getting meaning from a text also depends on the reader's purpose in reading it.

4.39 Readability formulae attempt to measure the difficulty of a text by assessing sentence length and the difficulty of its vocabulary. Although they can be useful screening tools, the results can be misleading.

4.40 Narrative is a particularly important structure that children exploit in making sense of texts. Some texts in school which purport to be narrative do not make it easy for children to use their understanding of narrative. Narrative form, if well done, can make knowledge more accessible.

4.41 Non-prose texts, especially worksheets, also depend on a range of conventions to convey meaning: spatial, linguistic, iconic, print, those that rely on world knowledge, and those that depend on 'school knowledge'. All of these can create difficulties for pupils.

4.42   Simplifying texts can make them easier to read, but it can also make them more difficult to read by making the text depend even more on implicit conventions.

4.43   Working actively with texts can help children to make sense of them and to become more familiar with the conventions they use.

4.44   Rather than a simpler text, a lesson sometimes needs more radical alteration to make it a meaningful experience for pupils. Learning from texts that children are unable to relate to the real world can be difficult.

5   THE LANGUAGE OF THE CLASSROOM

>CHILD (talking about the day at school): Mrs Megram showed us her essay today.
>
>FATHER: Oh yes? An essay about …
>
>CHILD: About 13 pages.
>
>FATHER: No, I didn't mean its length. Was it about teaching?
>
>CHILD: Yes.
>
>FATHER: Teaching what?
>
>CHILD: Teaching children!

5.1   Virtually all teaching involves the use of language to convey ideas and information, to assess what children understand, to control what happens in the classroom, and to evaluate children and their work. Some children appear better able than others to understand what their teachers say to them, to do what they are asked, and to use spoken language in the classroom for a variety of purposes: to describe, to recall, to classify, to compare, to predict, to direct, to reflect, to summarize, to question, to respond, and so on. Some children seem to be able to talk in the classroom in a more coherent way. Some children seem to command a wider vocabulary and more complex forms of language than others. Those who do not appear to be able to use language in ways that are expected of them, and to understand what their teachers say to them, are more likely to be described as having learning difficulties. In this section I am going to suggest that some of these difficulties for some of these children are avoidable. I shall argue that they arise from two sources in particular: the way in which language is associated with power in classrooms, and the conflicting assumptions of teachers and pupils as to how language may be used to talk about the world. In Section 4, I identified undeclared conventions in classroom texts as a source of difficulty and in this section, too, I shall analyse the ways in which undeclared conventions in the use of language can create problems for some children. It is important to stress that I am concerned here about the use of language as a medium through which learning takes place, not with the development of language *per se*.

THE IDEA OF LANGUAGE DEPRIVATION

5.2 The idea that difficulties can arise from the way teachers use language is not the only possible explanation for the apparent problems children face in using language effectively in school. Some teachers tend to attribute these problems to the language experience of children at home. They take the view that some children come to school lacking in essential language skills as a result of a deprived linguistic environment at home. When they come up against the language of the classroom they are unable to use language in the ways expected of them. This view is known as 'language deficit' or 'language deprivation' theory. Martin Hughes and Jacqui Cousins (1988) interviewed a sample of primary school headteachers and reception class teachers in Plymouth about the language problems of children starting school. The great majority of them subscribed to a form of language deprivation theory. The following quotations are typical:

> Parents don't talk to them ... it's all home really, isn't it ... sounds awful ... we get them straight from home so that's all you can blame it on.
>
> Language is the major problem. Children are unable to express themselves – they haven't done much talking at home. Conversation is not valued – nods and grunts are adequate for communication.
>
> (Quoted in Hughes and Cousins, 1988, p. 114)

5.3 The idea that some children – especially those from poor working-class homes – suffer at school because they come from homes where conversation doesn't happen often, or happens in a primitive form, is a recurrent belief in schools. In the 1960s and 1970s it was particularly influential in the development of preschool compensatory education programmes which aimed to teach children the language skills that they would need in order to cope at school. The theory has been the subject of a great deal of writing and research, and comes in many different versions. I shall mention three of the most common. A good source for those who want to know more is J. R. Edwards (1979).

5.4 At the crudest level, some proponents of deprivation theory – the teachers above, for example – argue that some children are simply not spoken to very often. Barbara Tizard and Martin Hughes (1984) observed and recorded the conversations of fifteen working-class and fifteen middle-class 4-year-old girls at home with their mothers. (They also observed them at their nursery schools; later in this section I shall refer to some of this evidence.) They found no evidence to support this version of the theory. Working-class mothers spoke as often and at equal length to their daughters as did middle-class mothers. A more detailed study by Gordon Wells and his colleagues (Wells, 1986) found the same.

5.5 More sophisticated versions of language deprivation theory hold that it is the difference between the uses and styles of language in the home that matters. Joan Tough (1977) contended that preschool children from disadvantaged working-class families were much less likely than middle-class children to use language for certain 'complex purposes' which are at a premium in school. Tough argued that these differences were the result of differences in the way that parents talked to their children. The middle-class children, she claimed, had more experience of these uses of language at home, and as a result were in a better position to use language in these ways at school. To test this claim, Tizard and Hughes counted the occasions when mothers made comparisons, recalled events, made future plans, linked events in time, gave reasons and made generalizations in conversation with their daughters. They found that all the mothers they studied used language in these ways, but middle-class mothers tended to use them more often than working-class mothers. But this does not mean that *all* middle-class mothers used language for complex purposes more than *all* working-class mothers. In fact there was a substantial overlap between the groups.

5.6 Another aspect of verbal deprivation theory that Tizard and Hughes examined concerns the use of explicit language. According to this view some parents encourage their children to be explicit more often than others, and since it is believed that children are expected to make their meanings explicit in classrooms, those who have become familiar with this requirement at home will be at an advantage at school. It is important to separate out the two parts of this theory. First is the claim that parents foster explicit talk to varying degrees. Second is the claim that explicit talk is required in school. Let's deal with the first part first. Conversation typically involves a great deal of implicit meaning. For example, standing in front of a television shop recently, I was asked by a stranger: 'What's the score?'. I knew immediately what he wanted to know. I was watching a football match, and it was obvious that he was interested in the score in that match at the moment. He did not need to say: 'What's the current score in the match you are watching?', and it would have been strange if he had. Most of his meaning was implicit. According to one version of language deprivation theory, propounded by the sociologist Basil Bernstein (1971), middle-class children gain greater experience than working-class children in making their language alone convey meaning, even when this is unnecessary.

5.7 Was there evidence in Tizard and Hughes' study that in middle-class homes children were more likely to be encouraged to be explicit?

> While there was in most respects no social class difference in the kind of 'cognitive demands' that mothers made, there was one exception. This was with respect to a group of very difficult demands which involved the child in reflecting on the basis of her statement – e.g., 'I don't know what you mean', 'How do you know?' and 'What do you mean?' Sometimes these questions were asked rhetorically. However, in our study, it was only the middle-class mothers who asked them with a pause, that is, an expectation that they would be answered ... However, although the mothers seemed to vary in the extent to which they encouraged

explicitness in their children, *all* the mothers became explicit themselves when they wanted to be sure that there was no misunderstanding.

(Tizard and Hughes, 1984, pp. 144–5)

So the evidence is at least equivocal. Some mothers encouraged their children to be explicit more than others, but all of them gave their children experience of being explicit when necessary. As to the second part of the theory – that classrooms are characterized by the use and understanding of explicit language – I shall come back to that later in the section, where I shall argue that it is completely mistaken.

5.8   There is little evidence to support the general proposition that working-class children suffer from language deprivation. This does not mean that there are not some children whose home language environment is seriously deprived. Some families are not conducive environments for children's development. But the very broad claims made by the teachers interviewed by Hughes and Cousins (1988) are not an adequate account of the difficulties some children encounter at school. That such views remain so common in the face of research evidence accumulated since the late 1960s is an interesting issue in its own right. These teachers are probably substantially underestimating the linguistic resources many of their children possess. But if the problems do not all arise from the children's language environment at home, then what is their source? Could they arise from the ways in which language is used in classrooms? We now have good reasons to look into the rather special ways in which language is often used in classrooms.

POWER AND CLASSROOM TALK

5.9   A classroom is a social setting quite unlike many others and very different from most children's experience of home. At home, children have a limited set of relationships to deal with. Their relationship to their parents is usually intimate, flexible and enduring. At school they have to relate to teachers in a much more formal and circumscribed manner. Opportunities to develop a close relationship are limited. They are in school for socially defined purposes, as are their teachers, who have responsibility for many children. Events take place according to tightly defined plans and have time slots allocated to them. All these features of the social organization of classrooms influence the way teachers and pupils talk to each other. None of the social characteristics of classrooms force teachers to behave in a particular way: classroom conversation varies a great deal. Nonetheless there are some recognizable features of talk in classrooms which are associated with their social structure. Classroom talk is often characterized by an uneven distribution of conversational power. In the next activity you will explore some of the properties and consequences of this. Note that I am not asking whether teachers are too powerful in schools, nor arguing for handing responsibility for the curriculum over to pupils. I am interested in how teachers' power is reflected in the ways they talk to children.

Activity 9 Dissecting conversational power

Read the following extract from a secondary school humanities lesson and write down the ways in which the teacher's power in the lesson is reflected in the dialogue. Look at what is said, but also think about how this conversation compares with more even-handed dialogues you have taken part in, for example, over the dinner table. As a useful supplementary exercise, you can do the same exercise on an extract from a whole-class discussion in any lesson you take part in. I give my comments below, but I urge you to do the exercise for yourself.

> T (TEACHER): Why do you think the creature [*an ammonite*] used to live inside a shell like that?
>
> P (PUPIL): (*numerous bids to speak next*)
>
> T: No, put your hands up please. Er, Carl?
>
> P: For protection.
>
> T: What does protection mean? Any idea, Carl?
>
> P: Sir, to stop things hurting it.
>
> T: Right, stops other things hurting it. Now if it came out of its shell, and waggled along the sea bed, what would happen to it? Yes?
>
> P: It might get ate.
>
> T: It might get eaten by something else, yeah. Um, why do you think this is made out of stone now? It's quite heavy, isn't it – weighs about a pound. It's a ... er, I won't tell you how a fossil happened yet, you'll be learning about that later, but why isn't – er, why don't we find the remains of the creature inside here?
>
> P: It would have rotted away.
>
> T: It would have rotted away. Why didn't the shell rot away?
>
> P: Sir, because it's too hard.
>
> T: It's too hard, good.
>
> (A. D. Edwards, 1980, p. 242)

5.10 This extract shows several ways in which the distribution of power between teacher and pupils in whole-class discussion can be uneven:

(a) Teachers have the right to define the topic of conversation, start a new topic, maintain a focus on the topic and bring it to a close. In this extract the teacher maintains tight control of the direction and structure of the conversation. The discussion has what I shall call a 'script', 'written' by the teacher. I have chosen this metaphor because of its theatrical nuances. This lesson, like many others, is carefully scripted in the way in which plays are, but with empty slots which are to be filled in by pupils. This is only one of a great many scripts that might be written about ammonites. Others, that the pupils might write, are out of the question. In order that the teacher can maintain control of the script, the empty slots must be filled with predefined responses.

(b) The teacher decides who talks when. Children are required to bid for the right to speak.

(c) The teacher defines the points at which children can contribute.

(d) The teacher has the right to evaluate, accept or reject contributions from pupils as relevant, irrelevant, correct or incorrect and has the power to correct mistakes.

(e) In most classroom talk, pupils have limited or no rights to challenge the adequacy of the teacher's explanations or the direction the lesson is taking. No challenges occur here. What would have been the response to 'Ah go on, tell us about fossils, sir'?

(f) The teacher asks many questions to which he already knows the answer. Every such question emphasizes the relative ignorance of the pupils.

(g) Pupils are allowed to respond to questions, but have little opportunity to take the initiative. When they do respond, they have only a very limited number of options open to them.

(h) Because the script for the lesson is written by the teacher, he is necessarily responsible for monitoring what happens in the discussion, and for intervening if something goes wrong, as when he corrects himself over the fossil point.

5.11 In what ways might the asymmetry of conversational power in a lesson such as this create learning difficulties for pupils? First, all pupils encounter exactly the same 'script'. As a system of communication, the lesson is inflexible. It cannot adapt easily to differences in the interests and understanding of the pupils. Second, if a pupil misses a point, or fails to understand, there are only limited opportunities to put the problem right. To do so, the pupil must make an unscripted intervention, and what amounts to a challenge to the adequacy of the teacher's explanations. This is not an easy option for a pupil to pursue. Third, the number of opportunities to contribute is limited by the teacher's script, so for much of the time pupils have to be passive listeners. They have little chance to talk about the ideas for themselves, to formulate their own understanding, to work on the material, to find out what they do and don't understand by talking about the ideas. Fourth, there are few opportunities for the teacher to discover just what pupils do and don't understand, since the opportunities for pupils to respond are so limited.

5.12 The asymmetry of conversational power in classrooms is not only reflected in whole-class discussions. We can also find it in one-to-one dialogues. Consider this conversation, taken from Tizard and Hughes' study, in which a nursery teacher talks to a 4-year-old who has asked for some help:

> JUNE: Can you cut that in half? Cut it in half?
>
> TEACHER: What would you like me to do it with?
>
> JUNE: Scissors.
>
> TEACHER: With the scissors? [*June nods*] Well, you go and get them, will you?
>
> JUNE: Where are they?
>
> TEACHER: Have a look round. [*June goes over to the cupboard, gets some scissors*] Where do you want me to cut it?
>
> JUNE: There.
>
> TEACHER: Show me again, 'cause I don't quite know where the cut's got to go. [*June shows teacher where she wants paper cut*] Down there? [*June nods; teacher cuts June's piece of paper in half*] How many have you got now? [1]
>
> JUNE: [*no reply*]
>
> TEACHER: How many have you got?
>
> JUNE: [*no reply*]
>
> TEACHER: How many pieces of paper have you got?
>
> JUNE: Two.
>
> TEACHER: Two. What have I done if I cut it down the middle?
>
> JUNE: Two pieces?
>
> TEACHER: I've cut it in … ? [*Wants June to say 'half'*]
>
> JUNE: [*No reply*]
>
> TEACHER: What have I done? [2]
>
> JUNE: [*No reply*]
>
> TEACHER: Do you know? [*June shakes head*]
>
> OTHER CHILD: Two.
>
> TEACHER: Yes, I've cut it in two. But … I wonder, can you think?
>
> JUNE: In the middle.
>
> TEACHER: I've cut it in the middle. I've cut it in *half*! There you are, now you've got two.

(Tizard and Hughes, 1984, pp. 194–5)

Activity 10 Half an idea

(a) What do you think the teacher's goals are in this conversation?

(b) What does it reveal about June's knowledge of the idea of 'a half'?

(c) What role does the teacher's conversational power play in the outcome of the dialogue?

5.13   The teacher seizes an opportunity offered by June's request for help to talk about the idea of halves and division by two. In doing so, June's practical purpose in talking to her teacher is replaced by her teacher's educational purpose. This may be June's first difficulty. She has quickly to shift her attention towards, and understand, a new conversational script. She has come to her teacher with a specific purpose, which is part of an activity in which she is engaged. To cope with her teacher's questions she has to put this to one side, and tune in to a new and unexpected activity. Note that the teacher neither needs nor seeks June's agreement for this shift, and does not signal the change explicitly. June is not in a position to challenge the new script, and indeed may lack the skill to do so.

5.14   It appears from the subsequent conversation that June does not know about halves. Yet it is clear from the first line of the conversation that she has no difficulty using the idea for her own purposes. Why then does she not answer her teacher's questions? Look at the two questions marked [1] and [2] in the extract. We interpret [1] 'How many have you got?' as referring to the two pieces of paper into which the original has been cut. But this is not made explicit until the question has been asked twice. Even when the teacher makes the meaning more explicit, it remains potentially ambiguous. Are there any other pieces of paper June is using apart from these? Is she supposed to include these in the calculation? We could interpret [2] 'What have I done?' as calling for the answer: 'You've cut it in half'. 'You've cut it in two' would normally be an acceptable answer as well, but the teacher has already indicated that this will not do by continuing the point after the other child has said 'Two'. Other possible answers to 'What have I done?' are: 'Used the scissors' or 'Cut it down the centre'. Notice that June does not make her confusion or uncertainty explicit by saying something like 'What do you mean?' or 'I don't know what you're on about'. It may be that she would find this difficult.

5.15   All this leads me to conclude that the evident difficulty in this dialogue is not the result of June's ignorance. I have suggested two other possible sources: the shift of script imposed by the teacher, and the implicit nature of the teacher's questions. The difficulty is produced by a conversation in which asymmetry of power is combined with teacher talk that is implicit and potentially ambiguous. I shall now look more systematically at implicitness and ambiguity in classroom talk. What kinds of ambiguity are we talking about here and what is their effect? What exactly is implicit in classroom conversations?

SHARED KNOWLEDGE AND MISCOMMUNICATION

5.16   As I said earlier, the need to refer to implicit assumptions in order to make sense of what someone says is not peculiar to classroom language. It is an essential part of the way we all talk. For example, some evenings in my own house, a conversation along these lines takes place:

A: Do you fancy some hot chocolate?
B: I've just had some coffee.
A: Look, I'm still finishing off this thing.
B: Alright, I'll get it.

This conversation is a successful attempt by A to persuade B to make her a cup of hot chocolate. How do the participants make sense of it? On the face of it, we should expect the answer to the first question to be 'yes' or 'no'. In order to understand the answer, we have to appeal to knowledge beyond what is said. The missing piece of information is: When B has just had a coffee, he doesn't want another drink. Understanding the meaning of the next utterance needs an appeal to further implicit knowledge: (a) when A asks B if he wants some hot chocolate late at night, it indicates that A wants some; (b) when A mentions hot chocolate and also says she is busy, this should be taken as a request for B to make it. The whole conversation works and achieves its purpose because A and B share an understanding of its purpose and an interpretation of each contribution.

5.17 The field of study which investigates such rules in conversation is known as discourse analysis, and a lot of attention has been devoted to the conventions of classroom discourse (Mehan, 1979; Edwards and Furlong, 1978; Edwards and Mercer, 1987). Derek Edwards and Neil Mercer (1987) have used the term 'educational groundrules' to describe the implicit assumptions that teachers make about the way in which questions, tasks and other aspects of classroom discourse are intended to be interpreted by pupils. You will see a link to the discourse conventions governing the interpretation of texts, which I discussed in Section 4.

5.18 I hope you can already see how far from the truth is the idea that classroom talk is a peculiarly explicit form of language. All the examples we have so far considered are full of implicit groundrules and conventions. Now if teacher and pupils do not share a common understanding of the groundrules for a conversation, the result is a miscommunication, and such miscommunications are often described as learning difficulties. They occur at a range of levels, from misunderstandings about single words, to much more fundamental gulfs between the groundrules of teacher and pupils. I am going to discuss three examples of miscommunications next, starting with a problem about a word, going on to a problem with a maths task, and then a case where very basic groundrules are not shared.

Example 1: Doing what comes naturally

5.19 I took part in a lesson in the 'language unit' of a primary school recently. The children were all statemented and had been placed there because of a range of difficulties that had been attributed to language or speech problems. The lesson was on 'Structures'. Each member of the group was given a chart divided into columns, one for each of a number of types of 'structure', such as 'metal', 'wood', and 'natural'. The teacher illustrated each category with some examples: a metal watering can, a wooden mirror, a plant. Darren was making little progress on his own, so I tried to get him started by asking if he could find something natural in the classroom. I had in mind that he might mention one of the plants, or the group's pet gerbil. He replied: 'Shoes'. I asked why shoes were natural, genuinely puzzled. 'Cos there's good for you. They're natural', he replied. Darren's understanding of the word 'natural' appears to be based on its use in advertising language – in such phrases as 'full of natural goodness'. It is not that he doesn't understand the word 'natural', but rather that his understanding and his teacher's understanding differ. To make progress his teacher needs to understand what Darren understands, to be able to say to Darren that natural can mean more than one thing, and to make explicit the teacher's meaning of the word. Classrooms need to be places where both teachers and children are able to identify and signal miscommunications, where they can both make what they mean and what they know explicit, and where there is an opportunity to relate conflicting understandings to one another.

Example 2: Divide and rule

5.20   Robert Hull is talking to B, the same child who had problems with the exercise in Figure 3. Here, B is struggling with some long divisions. Hull aims to find a meaningful way to talk about division:

> SELF: How much ice cream could you eat in one go?
>
> B: About this much. [*Hands describing amount*]
>
> SELF: All right, suppose I gave you four times that amount, four lots of it, how much would you be able to eat?
>
> B: I could eat it all.
>
> SELF: I thought you said you could only eat *that* amount. What about the rest?
>
> B: I could eat it later.
>
> (Hull, 1985, p. 100)

Are B's responses evidence of his ignorance of division? Hull thinks not: 'Either he is having me on, or it is a genuine intrusion of the empirical into my formal hypothetical question; he perhaps does not hear it as a maths question, about relations between amounts, but as a practical empirical question: what can be done with this huge amount of ice cream?' (Hull, 1985, p. 100). Hull argues that he and B do not share a common understanding of what the conversation is about. For Hull, the ice cream problem is to be interpreted as a maths problem. To work as such, the amount of ice cream that can be eaten at one go is a fixed 'given'. This is another example of what I described earlier as a school knowledge convention. But B's world knowledge seems to govern his interpretation of the conversation. It is a practical problem to which the solution is to save some of the ice cream until later. It is possible that B may have some relevant knowledge of division, but his interpretation of the dialogue ensures that it will not be revealed.

5.21   In another example, B reveals a sophisticated ability to deploy division in a practical context:

> SELF: All right, supposing ... how many times could you run round the school field, do you think?
>
> B: About twice.
>
> SELF: Supposing there was a field that was twice as far round as the school field, how many times do you think you could run round that?
>
> B: Once.
>
> SELF: If there was a field that was four times as far round as the school field, how many times do you think you could run round that?
>
> B: Half-way round ...
>
> (Hull, 1985, p. 101)

You may find it interesting to try to write down in mathematical terms what B must be doing to answer these questions. In the ice cream example and the extract from the conversation about halves, what looks like evidence of an individual child's difficulties turns out to be a failure by the two parties to establish a framework of agreed groundrules about the purpose and meaning of the dialogue. Classroom talk seems particularly vulnerable to such a lack of shared understanding.

5.22   The two examples we have considered so far have been rather specific in nature, to do with particular concepts. But some educational groundrules are rather more profound and pervasive. Consequently, the difficulties that arise when children do not come to terms with them may be especially serious. Next I am going to look at an example of the way in which these more pervasive groundrules can lead to learning difficulties. It happens to come from the USA, but the implications are not restricted by the Atlantic Ocean. I have not chosen this example because I think that it helps to explain some of the learning difficulties of a large number of children. Rather, my purpose is to show how features of classroom life to which we ordinarily pay little attention – characteristic ways of behaving, some of which might be described as part of the professional and personal identities of teachers – can be sources of learning difficulties for *some* children.

Example 3: Questions at home and at school

5.23   In school, children encounter questions that are characteristically educational. The most significant feature of such questions is that the questioner already knows the answer. And the person who is asked knows this. The purpose of the question is to get the child to display knowledge, or its absence. These questions are one of the devices I mentioned earlier which teachers use to keep control of the lesson's 'script'. Shirley Brice Heath (1982) studied the way in which questions were used in a school in a south-eastern part of the USA. Some of the children in the school came from a working-class black community called

Trackton, whose language uses she studied intensively. She compared the way in which children gained experience of questions in their own community with the way in which questions were used in conversation between the teachers at the school and with their own children at home.

5.24 In the teachers' homes, questions were a common part of children's conversational experience. In conversations with pre-verbal children, parents who were teachers often addressed children with questions and then supplied the answer, thus introducing them to the role of 'a question answerer'. In conversations with preschool-aged children, such parents continued to teach children to be 'answerers' by asking many questions to which the parents already knew the answer, such as 'Who's that?' or 'What colour is that?'. These questions frequently asked children to describe an attribute of an object, like its size or colour, or to label it. In Trackton, on the other hand, questions were not directed at children as often as in the teachers' homes. Young children were not seen as 'information-givers'. But this did not mean they were in any way linguistically deprived:

> ... their linguistic environment was rich with a variety of styles, speakers, and topics. Language input was, however, not especially constructed for them; in particular, they were not engaged as conversationalists through special types of questions addressed to them.

(Heath, 1982, p. 119)

In Trackton, questions which asked children to talk about the features of objects, people or pictures were rare. Much more often they were asked to make a comparison or an analogy between one object and another, with questions such as 'What's that like?'. On the rare occasions when teachers asked such questions in school they had in mind particular answers, but in Trackton, the children were free to make their own comparisons. Children often heard adults making comparisons and using metaphor in everyday conversation. As a result they became skilled 'comparers' from an early age. But they never offered, or were asked to provide, a definition of the attributes by which two things were similar.

5.25 Trackton children's experience of questions and their conversational competence at home was of little use in school, for they faced a new set of uses for questions. They were asked to name things, their parts and attributes; they encountered questions which checked their understanding. And many of the questions were about things of which they had no experience: 'to Trackton children, their teachers asked foreign questions about foreign objects' (Heath, 1982, p. 122). One boy encapsulated his problems precisely: 'Ain't nobody can talk about things being about theirselves' – i.e. that objects could not be described in terms of their own characteristics. In Trackton, children described objects by comparing them with others. By comparison with children whose preschool experience was full of school-like questions, Trackton children were at a considerable disadvantage and made less progress in school.

5.26 One solution to the failure of children to answer specific educational questions correctly has been to provide remedial programmes in which children are given 'sharply focused' training in specific skills such as identifying the colour and other characteristics of objects. Such programmes have been justified on the grounds that the children's performance in school suggests that they do not understand the concepts being taught. Children are taught to answer such questions as 'What colour is this?' and 'What shape is it?' in a direct fashion, so that if they fail to answer as required, they will be prompted with the right answer, and given practice by repeating it. But such programmes make extensive use of the very question types that Trackton children would have found so difficult. Heath argued that, whilst the Trackton children needed to learn how to cope with these questions, this could best be done by valuing and exploiting the skills that children already possessed.

5.27 Teachers began to introduce analogical, comparing questions into classroom conversation. Materials were introduced which were based on places and things that the children were familiar with, such as photographs of local buildings. Children were asked open-ended questions such as 'What's happening here?' and 'Have you ever been there?'. These discussions were taped and then teachers added to the tapes questions and answers about the names and attributes of objects. Trackton children enjoyed these tapes which provided a bridge between their own talk and classroom talk. Later on teachers asked Trackton children to join in the question-and-answer sessions, and they began to hear themselves responding successfully to classroom questions. As well as the tapes, teachers began to talk explicitly about questions and the kinds of answers that they required.

OVERCOMING MISCOMMUNICATION

5.28 Let's summarize. For much of their time in school some children make little sense of what is going on, and they lack the power, and possibly the skills, to say so. This happens because teachers assume that they share with their pupils certain ways of talking, certain implicit groundrules about what is meant when they talk, and a common purpose for their talk. And such assumptions may be quite mistaken. When communication breaks down, it is easy to misread the nature and source of the problem. A teacher may suppose that a child does not understand an idea, when the difficulty lies somewhere else entirely. Thus June appears not to understand the idea of a half, but she can use the word appropriately. What she doesn't understand is what her teacher wants her to say. A teacher may suppose that a child does not understand an idea when in fact the child does understand it, but what he understands isn't what his teacher understands. Thus what was 'natural' to Darren was not 'natural' to his teacher. A child may seem unable to use a skill, when in fact he is unable to use a skill in a particular task, because he cannot see the task as calling for that skill. Thus B can do division on the playing field but not with ice cream. Children may seem to have no relevant knowledge to bring to the classroom, when the problem is that there are no opportunities to display and use what they know. Thus Trackton children knew about questions, but their teachers did not know what they knew, and so could not make use of it.

5.29 It became customary in the 1980s to describe learning difficulties as a 'mismatch' between pupils and what they are expected to do. Now this word is open to many interpretations. Some authors have seen mismatch as a unidimensional business in which children are given tasks which are either too easy or too difficult. Neville Bennett and his colleagues conducted a large study of the 'match' (nicely ambiguous!) between primary-aged children and their curriculum (Bennett, Desforges, Cockburn and Wilkinson, 1984). They observed children at work and interviewed them to assess what they had learned. They claimed that more than half the tasks they observed were mismatched. They concluded in general that high attainers were given tasks which were too easy and low attainers were given tasks that were too difficult. Now, that tasks and children are sometimes mismatched is not in question. But the evidence I have discussed leads to the view that there is more to the problem than a single dimension of 'difficulty', as defined by the teacher. We need to understand the source of the difficulty; if we do not, we may fail to remove it, and instead make apparent simplifications that do nothing to simplify the task from the child's point of view. The paradoxical consequence of the miscommunications I have discussed is that teachers can simultaneously underestimate and overestimate what children know and can do. Children can be underestimated because miscommunication and asymmetry of conversational power prevents them from showing what relevant understandings they already have. And they can be overestimated in that their teacher fails to take into account their problems with the groundrules of classroom talk.

5.30 What are the implications of all this for practice? And how might classroom events be structured to avoid or overcome the miscommunications I have described? There are four broad implications. The first is that children need opportunities to bring their own existing knowledge and understanding into play in lessons, so that the teacher can understand what they understand, so that they can relate what they already know to what they are learning and so that they can work actively towards new understandings. The second is that teachers need to be open-minded interpreters of children's activity. The third is that teachers need to be aware of the implicit groundrules that they use, and the potential for learning difficulties that they create. The fourth is that the classroom needs to be an environment in which misunderstanding and miscommunication surface as quickly as possible, and do not remain unrecognized. What these broad implications mean in practice will be discussed in the rest of this double unit.

A case study: primary science

5.31 To begin the task, I shall finish this section with a practical account of some ways in which children's existing understandings can be included in lessons. In science education, a great deal of work has been done in understanding the way in which children understand scientific concepts. Children's notions of such terms as 'force' and 'energy' have turned out to be significantly different from what their teachers often believe them to be. In the next reading, Pamela Wadsworth explains the work of one project which has investigated primary school children's scientific ideas. She describes and illustrates the methods that teachers involved in the project have used to encourage children to express their existing ideas about scientific concepts.

Activity 11 Starting from children's ideas

Now read 'Primary science: starting from children's ideas' by Pamela Wadsworth (Reader 1, Chapter 4). You will find that the chapter picks up a number of the ideas already discussed. You may find it useful to identify these connections. I shall comment on the chapter under the headings of the four points I identified in paragraph 5.30.

Bringing children's ideas into play

5.32   This chapter offers several strategies for enabling children to express their ideas. These include talk in small groups. In Section 7, I shall look more closely at how small-group talk can work, and give some illustrations which include children described as having moderate learning difficulties. Wadsworth shows how the form in which children express their ideas affects what they can express. Thus some children found it difficult to say what a shadow is, but they had no difficulty in drawing one. In the discussion of B and division, we saw the way in which context could aid or prevent children from using their knowledge. In that example, the limiting factor was B's interpretation of the purpose of the conversation. We also saw in para. 5.12 how conversational context prevented June from revealing her understanding of 'a half'. Wadsworth has introduced another aspect of context and its impact on how children reveal what they know: the ideas children can express depend on their having the means with which to do so. The contexts available to children to express their ideas are clearly very important in understanding what children know and don't know. In Unit 8/9 we shall return to this point when we look at the significance of the National Curriculum for understanding and assessing children's learning.

Interpreting children's ideas

5.33   I said that teachers need to be open-minded interpreters of children's activity. This chapter begins to discuss what this means. In her discussion of children's comments on rusting and evaporation, Wadsworth shows how children's ideas are often open to a range of interpretations. It is often impossible to arrive at definitive theories to explain them. There is an interesting comparison to be made between the activity of the children, in interpreting the causes of events like rusting, and the activity of teachers in explaining children's interpretations. Some of the children Wadsworth quotes are willing to be provisional and to avoid hasty conclusions. And they seek reason and order in what they are investigating. Are teachers similarly willing to be provisional in interpreting children's ideas? Are they generally disposed to look for the orderliness in these ideas which Wadsworth reveals? Who is the better scientist? In Section 6, I shall discuss and illustrate the place of interpretation by the teacher in teacher–pupil dialogue.

Groundrules and misunderstanding

5.34 In this chapter we can see further examples of the way in which implicit assumptions about language use may create problems for children. Many scientific terms have ordinary language meanings as well. Wadsworth gives the example of 'light'. Children bring with them these ordinary language uses, and it will be these ideas that they draw on in lessons, not an undeclared scientific meaning that the teacher has in mind. Darren's use of 'natural' is a case in point. Another groundrule for science that Wadsworth discusses is that it seeks to explain things which need explanation. She points out that children may not see the need for an explanation of, for example, how we see things. If children do not see something as a puzzle, then the purpose of the lesson will be obscure. But children are often better at seeing puzzles than adults. Growing up in our society can involve learning not to be curious.

Making misunderstanding public

5.35 In the last section of the chapter, Wadsworth discusses the kind of classroom environment that will encourage children to make explicit what they do (and don't) know. In Section 7, I shall take up this issue when I look at the development of collaborative learning environments.

SUMMARY

5.36 Some writers and teachers have attempted to explain the language difficulties that children have in school in terms of a deprived language environment at home. It has been argued that many children are not spoken to often, are not encouraged to use language for 'complex purposes', or are not helped to make their meaning explicit. The language environment of families does vary, and some children do lack linguistic stimulation at home. But many children who seem to have difficulties using language at school have rich language environments at home. Some difficulties involve the way language is used in school.

5.37 In classroom conversations power is often unevenly distributed. The power of teachers to define the purpose, topic and structure of talk in lessons can create difficulties by forcing all pupils to deal with the lesson in the same way, by limiting their ability to say when they don't understand, and by forcing them into passive roles.

5.38 Communication in classrooms depends on teacher and pupils sharing an understanding of the implicit assumptions made about the way language is used. When this condition is not met, confusion in pupils can result, and it is often referred to as a learning difficulty. The source of difficulty may be unrecognized or misunderstood by the teacher, and pupils may find it difficult to say what the problem is.

5.39 Children need to be able to bring their existing knowledge and understanding to bear on what they learn, and to work at new ideas actively. This allows them to formulate new knowledge for themselves and to relate it to what they already think. It also allows their teacher to see better what they understand, and the way it differs from what he or she understands.

6 DIVERSIFYING LESSONS

6.1 So far I have examined the learning difficulties that can arise from texts and from language use in classrooms, and I have begun to discuss strategies for circumventing some of these difficulties. In this section I shall turn to difficulties that are created by the way in which tasks and lessons are organized, and look at forms of organization aimed at minimizing learning difficulties. I shall begin with the problems generated when all children are expected to do the same tasks. Then I shall look at one popular solution to these problems: the individualization of learning. I shall discuss the benefits as well as the drawbacks of this approach. Then, in the core of this section, I am going to look at how lessons can be organized to respond to diversity through the use of a wider variety of relatively open-ended tasks to which pupils can respond in a range of ways. I shall use secondary mathematics as my main example. As part of this section you will watch TV4 *Rich Mathematical Activities*. Make sure that you read the section up to Activity 13 before watching the programme.

HETEROGENEOUS GROUPS, HOMOGENEOUS TEACHING

6.2 Every classroom contains children who will approach learning tasks from a variety of starting points. This is as true of classes in special schools as it is of classes in mainstream schools. Of course, the degree of pupil diversity in a class depends on the grouping methods used by the school. Schools which set or stream pupils do produce more homogeneous classes than schools which do not. But this does not mean that ability grouped classes have identical attainments; such a group of pupils does not exist. The introduction of in-class support for children who experience learning difficulties has often increased the diversity of pupils in classes. What happens if a class is taught in a way that fails to take its diversity into account?

6.3 Some varieties of whole-class teaching are unresponsive to diversity. In Section 4, I examined the impact of the asymmetry of power in classroom language, and my first example was an extract from a whole-class lesson. I pointed to the problems that can be generated when all the children in a class encounter the same 'lesson script' from which they are unable to deviate. You might wish to remind yourself of the points that emerged from the analysis of the humanities lesson in Activity 9. I argued that the lack of flexibility, the limited opportunities for pupils to make misunderstandings public, the passivity required of pupils and the lack of access for the teacher to pupils' developing ideas were all potential sources of difficulty for some children. Now this is not a case for the abandonment of whole-class teaching. The problems do not result from the fact that a whole class is being addressed collectively by a teacher, but from the uniform, predetermined script of a lesson. A whole-class session need not have a predetermined script at all. Alan Howe (1988) provides a valuable account of how whole-class sessions can be used to enable diverse groups to participate and gain confidence and practice in public talk.

6.4 Activity 9 revealed some of the immediate difficulties created by teaching which assumes homogeneity. A study by John Ingram and Norman Worrall (1990) looked at some of the longer term consequences. Ingram and Worrall studied junior classes with teachers described as 'highly directive in all activities'. In one classroom they asked the teacher and children to record the activities they did each day. Children were generally accurate at doing this. The two resulting accounts of activities did not concur. In one five-week spell the teacher recorded twenty 'periods' of English. Pupils recorded between none and seventeen periods. Paradoxically, in classrooms where work was apparently tightly controlled by the teacher, Ingram and Worrall found a substantial gap between what the teacher thought was happening and what the children were actually doing:

> The comments from the teachers indicated that they were in some sense unaware of what was really happening in the classroom. That is, they had a perception of children if not doing the current lesson at least 'about to start' or 'having just finished' ...
>
> (Ingram and Worrall, 1990, p. 60)

6.5 What were the children's perceptions? Ingram and Worrall talked to a group of 7- to 11-year-olds from four 'directive' classrooms in order to find out. They asked: 'Do you find keeping up with your lessons very easy, very hard or just right?' They called children who found it very hard to keep up 'backmarkers'. Children who found it very easy were called 'frontrunners'. Backmarkers, who were the majority of the children, generally avoided telling their teacher they were behind. If they had not finished their work in the time allotted, the most common response was to let the backlog build up. Most did not take active steps to clear it. Backmarkers were not happy about their position. They said things like 'I'm useless', 'I feel thick' and 'I don't feel good':

> The cumulative consequence of such a regime was that weaker children would each day develop an increasing backlog of work, thereby setting demands which could not be met for time reasons alone, even assuming the child were able enough. This backlog phenomenon does therefore seem again a significant part of the hidden curriculum, and it was clear from asking the children that negative self-concepts were being formed, and a sense of strain and in some cases even hopelessness comes out in their answers.
> (Ingram and Worrall, 1990, p. 61)

6.6 In this account, teaching which assumes that all children have similar learning needs emerges as a source of substantial difficulty for a large proportion of children. It is compounded by the fact that teachers appeared not to realize the extent to which children were falling behind. Now one possible solution would be to slow down the pace at which the class is expected to work, or to pitch the lessons at a lower level. But the penalty for this may be to exchange the sense of failure of some pupils for the frustration of others. The challenge is to find forms of organization which enable children to work in ways appropriate to them, and which will allow all of the members of a class to make progress. How can this happen in a mixed-ability class, and happen in a way that is practicable, which enables the teacher to plan coherently and monitor pupils' progress? For some teachers in primary schools, this may seem a strange question to ask. Nearly all primary classes are unstreamed, and frequently not grouped by ability within the class. In many classrooms children are used to working in different ways at different tasks. But in secondary schools, homogeneous whole-class teaching remains a common strategy. It is for this reason that this section concentrates on the secondary age range.

INDIVIDUALIZED LEARNING

6.7 Some writers argue that the answer to the problems of mixed-ability teaching lies in individualized learning. Graham Upton, for example, sees it as the only alternative:

> If children are experiencing difficulties in any aspect of school learning it is vital that any work which is provided for them is at an appropriate level of difficulty ... Unless you are faced with a homogeneous group of children, this means that work must be individualized.
> (Upton, 1989, p. 202)

6.8 Many teachers have spent a great deal of effort producing worksheets pitched at various levels so that children could work at tasks matched to their attainments. One common approach has been the development of a core of material, which all children in a class are expected to cover, with extension material for children making rapid progress, and adapted or simplified versions of the material for lower attainers.

6.9 Individualization has been widely used in mathematics, particularly since the advent of commercially available banks of graded workcards. With these materials, lessons organized around whole-class presentation and exercises are replaced by lessons in which children may be working on the same topic area, but they will use a range of different workcards or booklets at different levels. As they work through the scheme they and their teacher keep a record of progress. The teacher becomes a resource manager, a monitor of pupil progress, and an individual tutor. Whole-class work is not necessarily abandoned altogether: certain topics may need discussion with the class, but it ceases to be the principal strategy for teaching new material.

6.10 In their account of developments at Whitmore High School (Reader 2, Chapter 2) Christine Gilbert and Michael Hart describe the introduction of mixed-ability teaching of mathematics through individualized materials, and you may wish to look briefly at this now to refresh your memory. Other accounts of the same change in the way mathematics is taught at secondary level are offered by Kyne (1987) and Fleming, Dadswell and Dodgson (1990). Where individualization has been used to replace ability grouping with mixed-ability work, teachers have noted a reduction in the adverse effects of selection and labelling. They have observed improvements in the confidence and independence of children who had experienced earlier difficulties in whole-class taught lessons. Individualization also gives an active role to learning support teachers, who can monitor and support individuals during lessons on equal terms with subject teachers.

6.11 But there are limitations as well. Individualization throws a heavy burden on the materials as the main teaching device, and therefore raises all the issues I discussed in Section 4. It reduces contact between teacher and pupils, so that there are only limited opportunities to deal with misunderstandings. It can limit variety of response in lessons, so that children are doing similar tasks from one lesson to the next. It calls for extremely tight organization of materials, it can add great pressure on time if extra materials have to be developed, and it can force skilled teachers into a rather limited administrative role. It prevents pupils from using one of the most valuable resources of the classroom: each other. Without an audience, children are not encouraged to formulate their own understanding actively, and they miss opportunities to learn from the ideas of their peers.

DIVERSIFICATION

6.12 In the rest of this section I am going to investigate how lessons might be organized for diversity so that they avoid the limitations of individualization. I am going to discuss some examples of work in one subject area – mathematics – to show how what I shall call 'diversification' can work in practice. An alternative, excellent account of diversifying lessons (though she does not use this term) is provided by Susan Hart (1989), who uses humanities as her example.

6.13 My account of the practical effects of diversifying lessons draws particularly on the work of two teachers, both of whom work with children who experience difficulties in learning, but in different contexts. When the course was in preparation, Adrienne Bennett was a teacher at Watergate School, a special school on the Isle of Wight for children identified as having moderate learning difficulties. Barbara Miller was the head of maths at Tideway School, a comprehensive school in East Sussex. Adrienne and Barbara shared a common approach to teaching mathematics which was influenced by the work of two curriculum development projects; the Low Attainers in Mathematics Project (LAMP) and the Raising Achievement in Mathematics Project (RAMP). These projects were concerned to improve the quality of teaching and learning in secondary mathematics, especially for low-attaining pupils. The work of the LAMP project, the first of the two, is reported in Ahmed (1987). These two projects have worked from a set of basic arguments about teaching and learning mathematics, and the sources of difficulties in doing so:

(a) Mathematics is more than a body of knowledge – a collection of facts, rules and techniques. It is also an activity in which people engage by observing, speculating, predicting, hypothesizing, testing, generalizing, proving, etc. Children need to engage in these activities if they are to understand and give meaning to mathematical knowledge. To use the language of the late 1980s/early 1990s, children need to engage in mathematical activity if they are to 'gain access' to mathematics.

(b) The mathematical diet of pupils with learning difficulties is often restricted to tightly sequenced learning of basic skills in an attempt to simplify the problems for pupils. This approach is itself a source of learning difficulty if it produces unfulfilling, monotonous tasks for which children can see no purposes, and are not committed to. Instead, children need 'challenges to get their teeth into' (Ahmed, 1987, p. 14).

(c) Many mathematics classrooms are 'answer-oriented', that is, the aim of tasks is to 'get the right answer', rather than understand the mathematics of the task. Pupils depend on the teacher to tell them whether or not they are working appropriately. They are not encouraged to evaluate their own progress, use their own powers of reasoning, and relate what they are learning to what they already know. Teachers often pre-empt children's own thinking to prevent them 'getting in a mess'. The result is that 'getting the right answer' actually inhibits mathematical development. (We can see another version of the teacher-controlled lesson script here.)

Activity 12 Opening up learning in a special school

Now read 'What will happen if … ? An active approach to mathematics teaching', by Adrienne Bennett with Honor Williams (Reader 1, Chapter 5). In this chapter, Adrienne gives an account of her work with a class of Year 10 and 11 pupils in Watergate School. As you read it, make a list of the features of the way in which Adrienne works with her class under the following headings:

(a) the organization of lessons;

(b) the tasks set;

(c) how pupils are active participants.

These headings do not exhaust the material in the chapter, so do focus as well on other aspects that interest you.

Organization of lessons

6.14 Adrienne uses a combination of whole-class, individual and group work. (As in most special schools, her class is small.) But pupils are not obliged to work as a group if they do not find it helpful. One of the aims of group or pair work is to increase the flexibility of lessons, so requiring children to collaborate would seem contradictory.

The tasks set

6.15 The idea of a 'rich mathematical activity' is at the heart of Adrienne Bennett's (and, as we shall see, Barbara Miller's) work:

- Activities are rich in two senses: in their mathematical possibilities, and in the range of choices they leave open to pupils as to how they tackle the task. This is well illustrated by the range of enquiries that developed from the Fibonacci sequence of numbers.

- Tasks are sufficiently open-ended to require decisions from pupils themselves about the questions they will ask and the limitations they will set. Pupils help to define the terms of the problem. This investment helps to develop a commitment to the task.

- Pupils have opportunities to work on tasks through practical activity, talking and writing.

- Tasks are not presented in such a way that pupils either succeed or fail. Every idea from a pupil can be a useful contribution on which development can be based, thus the nature of the task allows pupils' ideas to be valued.

- Tasks give a sense of purpose to pupils' work. This can carry over a number of lessons, so pupils' experience is not fragmented.

- Tasks provide reasons for pupils to deploy and develop their mathematical skills, including basic number skills.

- Tasks do not depend extensively on recall of facts, or on the ability to read or write.

Pupils as active participants

6.16 Pupils are active in many ways: they see problems as mathematical, as in John's padlock; they make decisions about how to tackle problems; they define, explore and solve problems; they speculate and predict; they test out predictions by collecting evidence; they search for and find patterns; they explain and justify; they record and report their thinking at early provisional stages as well as at later stages.

TV3 *RICH MATHEMATICAL ACTIVITIES*

6.17 Adrienne Bennett works with a small group of pupils who have already been selected on the basis of low attainment, so one might argue that diversifying lessons and tasks is easier than it would be in a mainstream mixed-ability class of thirty or so pupils, especially if it contained pupils who might otherwise attend a school like Adrienne's. In TV Programme 3 this is one of the issues we shall explore.

BEFORE THE PROGRAMME

6.18 In this programme you will see Adrienne Bennett and Barbara Miller at work. We filmed Barbara Miller working with a first-year and a second-year class, both of them mixed ability. In the second-year class, you will also see Barbara Ritchie, one of the teachers who provide learning support in mathematics at Tideway School. Adrienne Bennett was filmed working with the same class at Watergate School that she describes in Reader 1, Chapter 5.

6.19 The programme is divided into four short sections, each covering a different mathematical activity. If you have time, you will gain more from the programme if you explore the mathematical activities for yourself before watching. I have included several questions you might investigate.

Baked bean tins

6.20 In the first section of the programme, you will see a mixed-ability, first-year class working with Barbara Miller on an activity called 'baked bean tins'. There are two aims in watching this section:

(a) to show how the organization of the class, and provision of a rich activity, allows for varying responses from different pupils;

(b) to see how the dialogue between teacher and pupil works in a diversified lesson.

Picture a stack of tins on display in a supermarket. On the top, there is one tin, on the next row, two tins, then three, four, five, etc. How many tins are there in a stack with one, two, three, four, twenty, fifty rows? How many tins are there in a stack with n rows? Is there a general formula which links the number of rows and the number of tins in a stack? The stack of tins is a useful model for the sequence of 'triangular numbers' 1, 3, 6, 10, 15, 21. The numbers in this series are sums of consecutive whole numbers from 1 onwards:

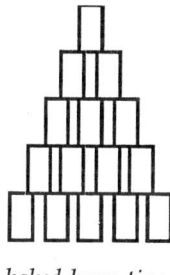

$3 = 1 + 2$

$6 = 1 + 2 + 3$

$10 = 1 + 2 + 3 + 4$

and so on.

baked bean tins

6.21 You will see the challenges that the activity presented to two pupils, Matthew and Mark, and the way in which Barbara supported them. These two boys work at very different levels within the same activity. What makes this possible? How does Barbara support these pupils?

Triangles

6.22 Next we move to Adrienne Bennett. There are two aims in watching this section:

(a) to see how pupils in this class of children with 'moderate learning difficulties' use the choice that they have within the activities Adrienne provides;

(b) to see how the control that pupils have affects their dialogue with the teacher.

First you will see Lisa investigating patterns of 'number triangles'. The number in the centre is the sum of three numbers at the apexes. Adrienne showed the class an example on the board, and left it to them to explore possibilities. We see Lisa after she has been developing her work for about an hour.

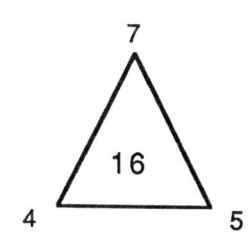

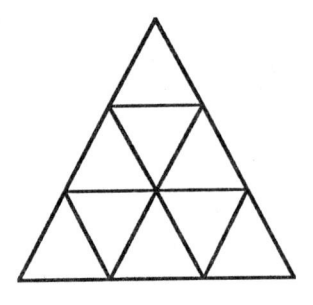

6.23   Then we see another pupil, Shane, working in the same lesson on a different activity. Shane and Ian chose to explore patterns in triangle 'piles', built from match sticks. There are a lot of possibilities here. How many small triangles are there in each row? Is there a rule for the way the number in each row grows as you add extra rows to the bottom of the pattern? How many small triangles are in the pile as a whole? How many triangles are there in a pile with two, three, four, five, ... rows? What numbers do you get if you write out this series? Shane and Ian began by writing out the series of numbers of triangles in each row, and they noticed how the pattern was constructed. At this point Adrienne joined them and decided to extend their work by setting a new challenge: How many triangles are in a pile with one, two, three or more rows? What does this series look like?

Maxbox

6.24   Next we return to Tideway School, this time to a second-year, mixed-ability class in the second lesson of an activity called Maxbox. In this section concentrate on two points:

(a) the role of a learning support teacher;

(b) how the organization of the lesson fosters collaboration between pupils.

Maxbox is an activity that involves working with the volume of cuboids. You have a 10 cm × 10 cm square piece of paper. You cut four small squares out of the corners, and fold the paper into an open box.

What is the volume of the box? Could you make a box with a larger volume with the same size piece of paper? What size of square, cut out from the corners, will give the largest possible volume?

6.25   In this lesson, you will see two groups of pupils:

(a) Chris and Brian, working with learning support teacher, Barbara Ritchie. Chris is using the activity to develop a better understanding of volume. Brian is working on volume as well, but he encounters difficulties in drawing a 'net' on paper, which will then fold into a box when it is cut out.

(b) Claire, Demelza, Leonie and Lyndsey, working with Barbara Miller. These girls are calculating the volume of boxes using cut-outs measured in whole and half centimetres, and testing a hypothesis about which cut-outs will give the largest volume for pieces of paper of more than one size.

The triangle water game

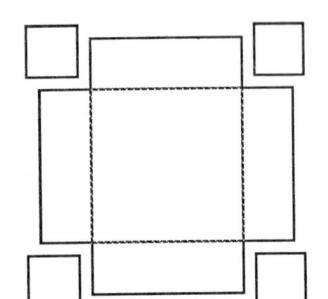

6.26   In the final part of the programme we return to Adrienne Bennett's class for an activity that occupied the class for a whole morning. This part provides a brief glimpse into another kind of collaboration, and some of the mathematics that emerged. The activity had been brought in by one of the class, Michael, who had bought a 'water game' while he was on holiday. It is shown in Figure 6. Nine equilateral triangular shapes, three blue and six pink, can be moved around in the liquid-filled space between two perspex sheets, using a plunger. They land on a platform and the object of the game is to build them into a larger equilateral triangle. At home, Michael had set himself the task of finding out how many different arrangements of three blue and six pink triangles he could make. The class takes up this challenge.

Activity 13 Rich Mathematical Activities

Now watch the programme (TV3). If you can record it to watch again later you will get more out of it. Here is a summary of points to concentrate on:

- Baked bean tins: the different responses Mark and Matthew make to the task. How Barbara supports both pupils.

- Number triangles and equilateral triangle patterns: the quality of the interaction between teacher and pupils.

- Maxbox: pupil collaboration, and the roles of class and support teacher.

Figure 6 The triangle game

DIVERSITY IN PRACTICE

6.27 In all the lessons we filmed for this programme, pupils were at work in an enormous range of different individual tasks chosen within the activities provided by the two teachers. What you saw on the film is a tiny fraction of the whole. In the baked bean tins investigation, I asked you to concentrate on the responses from Matthew and Mark. The activity provided these two boys with quite different challenges.

6.28 Matthew's first challenge was to construct a representation of the problem he was working on. In his last maths lesson before we filmed, Matthew drew five stacks accurately on paper, shown in Figure 7. He recorded a significant discovery: 'I find out that if we don't have gupas [gaps] it would not work'. Without drawing the stack, he wrote that eight layers would contain 36 tins. Barbara's dialogue with Matthew during this lesson continued on 'dialogue sheets' attached to his work. These sheets allowed Barbara to comment on the work. Some pupils also use them to communicate with her. They are rather like the Open University's PT3 forms! Barbara wrote on Matthew's dialogue sheet: 'Well done for predicting eight levels. Can you write about how you did it? Could you work out how many tins would be in 20 levels?' This question prompted the work that you saw in the programme. Matthew had been able to draw smaller stacks on paper last week, and wrote about the need for 'gaps'. In this lesson, before Barbara's intervention, the gaps had been forgotten, the shape was transformed, and the rule that each successive layer should have one more tin that the last was abandoned. Why? It

'It'll go 20, 10, 9, 8, 7, 6, …'

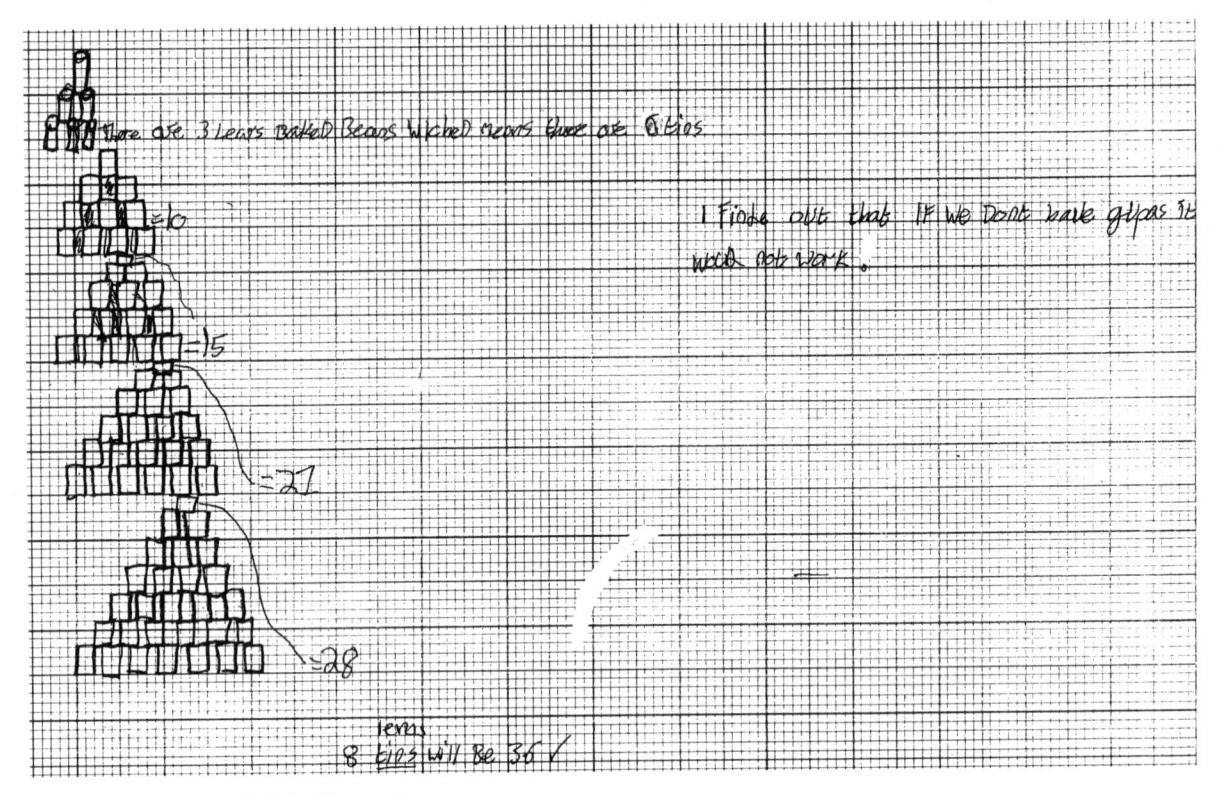

Figure 7   Matthew's baked bean tins

may have been the larger numbers Matthew was now working with, or possibly the multilink cubes. Whatever the cause, Matthew's representation of the problem is clearly very context-sensitive. Continued practical activity was therefore important in allowing him to develop a more resilient understanding. However, his work is not restricted to practical activity. Later in the lesson, having understood more clearly the nature of the problem, he performed and recorded the calculation accurately. Then he set himself the next challenge:

> I add 20 to 1. The answer was big so I wonder what would the answer be 100 to 1.

'Unfortunately it's the height that you know, so could you do that round the other way?'

6.29   Mark worked at a different level, and faced different challenges. He and Matthew began at the same point. Both of them calculated the number of tins in stacks of one up to seven layers. But Mark then searched for, and found, a relationship between the number of tins and the number of layers, which he expressed in a table, shown in Figure 8. This formed the basis for the dialogue with Barbara that we filmed. In that conversation Mark discovered the rule that links the height of the stack to the number of tins, and afterwards, he recorded this in a progressively abstract and formal manner, shown in Figure 9. In later lessons, and for homework, Mark chose to explore rules for related series.

6.30   The comparison between Matthew and Mark's work highlights some of the ways in which diversification occurs in Barbara's work:

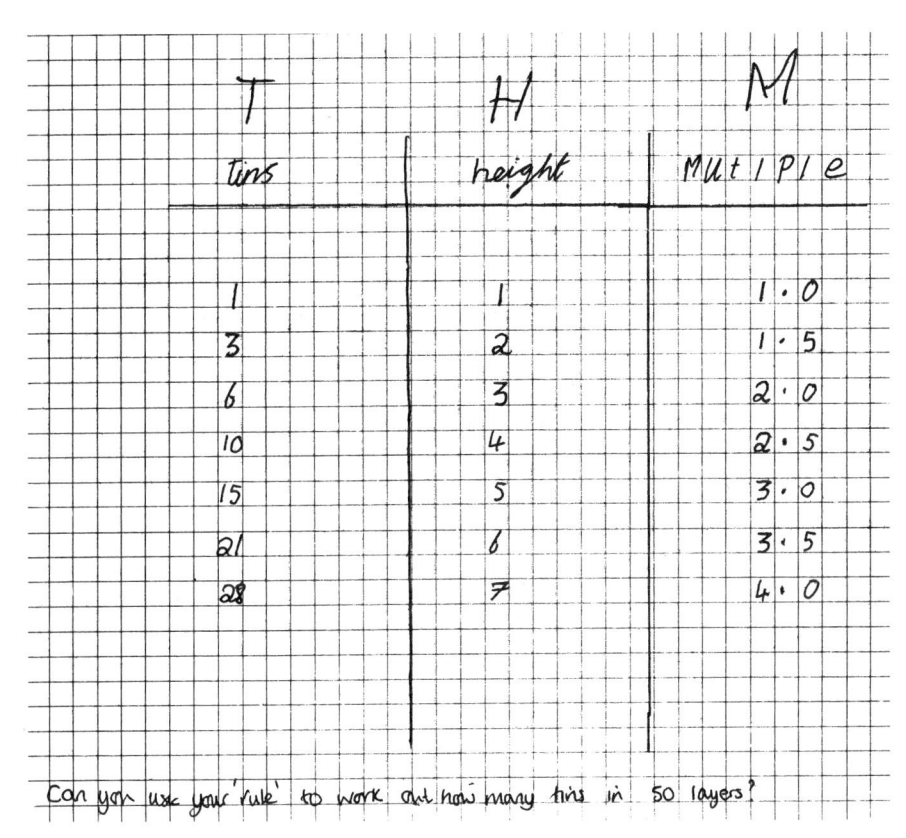

T	H	M
tins	height	Multiple
1	1	1.0
3	2	1.5
6	3	2.0
10	4	2.5
15	5	3.0
21	6	3.5
28	7	4.0

Can you use your 'rule' to work out how many tins in 50 layers?

Figure 8 Mark's baked bean tin table

- the activity is accessible to everyone in the class, that is, all pupils can see the purpose of the activity; it does not require a complicated explanation; no reading is involved;
- for children who make rapid progress the activity is extendable;
- pupils choose what specific tasks they will explore within the activity; there is not one common end-point that all pupils are expected to reach, nor is there a teacher-defined set of steps that all pupils have to work through;
- pupils choose how to record their work;
- teacher support is based on understanding what pupils are trying to achieve, the difficulties they face, and the next mathematical steps they can take.

6.31 In choosing to concentrate on Matthew and Mark, I may have given the impression that the result of diversifying lessons is only to allow children to respond to a task at different 'levels'. This can give the impression that differences between pupil responses can all be ranked into levels. But if we look at Adrienne Bennett's class, we can see that the pupils' responses differ in ways that cannot be ranked so easily. In effect, the children define and carry out different tasks.

A simpler rule is two sind the height that you want, add 1 ~~this~~ and then you divide by 2 and you will get the amount you have to multiply by.

Good — this is clearly explained, but can we write this in a shorter way?

Height + 1 ÷ 2 = Anwser ×

((Height + 1) ÷ 2) ~~×~~ *× by height = tins*

((H + 1) ÷ 2) × H = T

Clearly expressed.

Figure 9 Mark's baked bean tin formula

'What are these at the top: E, O, E, O?'

6.32 Lisa's work on number triangles illustrates the process. This is shown in Figure 10. It is remarkable for the range of patterns and relationships it contains. Lisa herself found and recorded the alternate columns of odd and even numbers which Adrienne discussed with her in the programme. There is much else to discuss:

- The totals in each row increase by one; the totals in each column increase by two. Why?

- The first column in the first set of numbers produces all even results. Why? Has it anything to do with the composition of the triples? You might notice that every triple in this column consists of two odd numbers and an even number. What about the second column?

- If you look at the diagonals in the first set you will see rows of the same results: two eights, two nines, three tens, etc. Are there more ways to make ten with three numbers chosen from the first nine positive whole numbers?

- There are 28 triangles in the first block, and 21 in the second. Could you predict the number of triangles in the block with a 3 at the top of each triangle? What if you put a zero at the top? Could you do that?

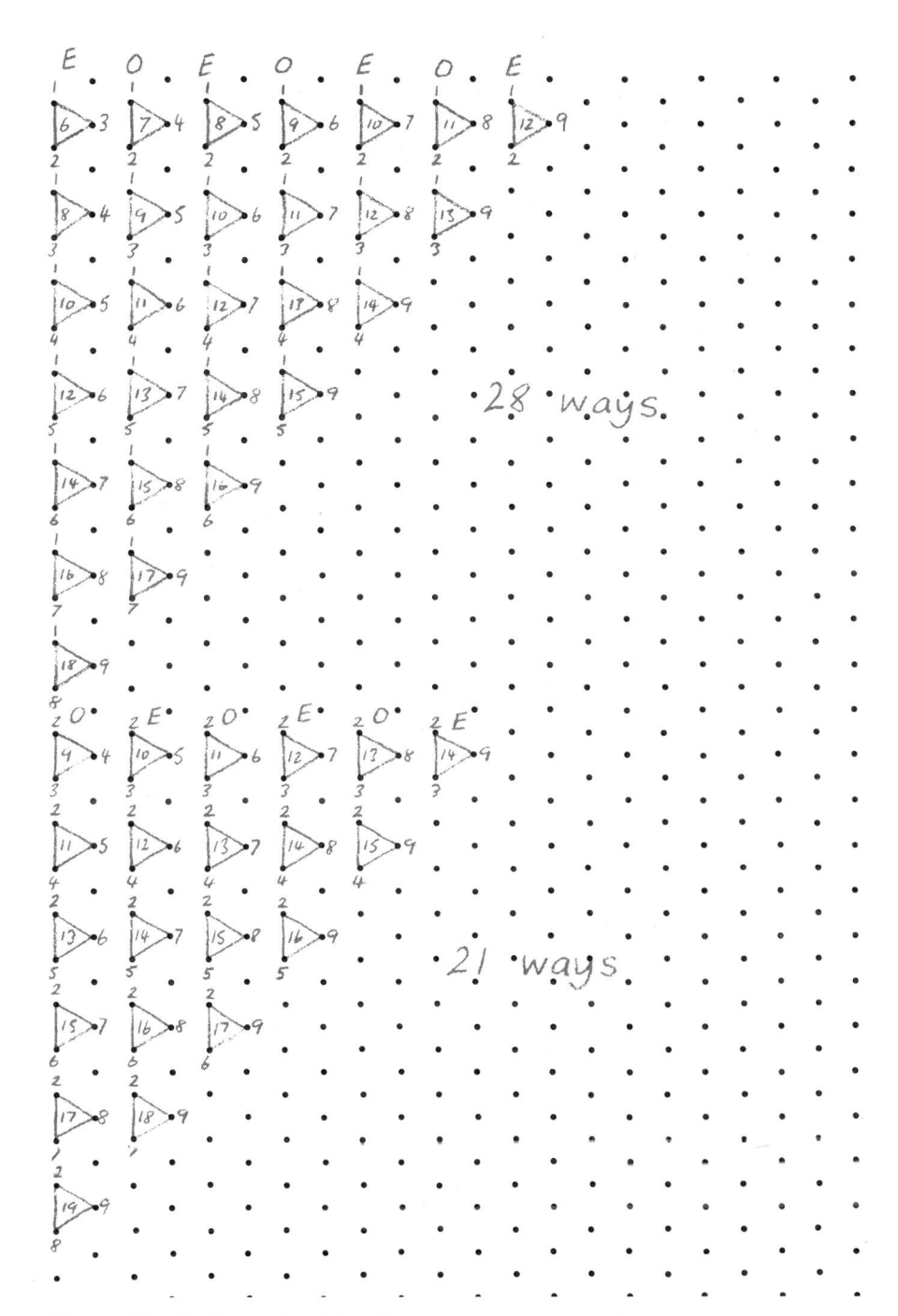

Figure 10 Lisa's number triangles

6.33   Apart from the beautiful structure in Lisa's work, there is also the simple fact that she is exercising her basic arithmetic skills with gusto. Shortly before we filmed, Lisa had written that 'doing pages of sums is boring'. Yet she devoted more than an hour to the number triangles. What made the difference?

Number triangles

+

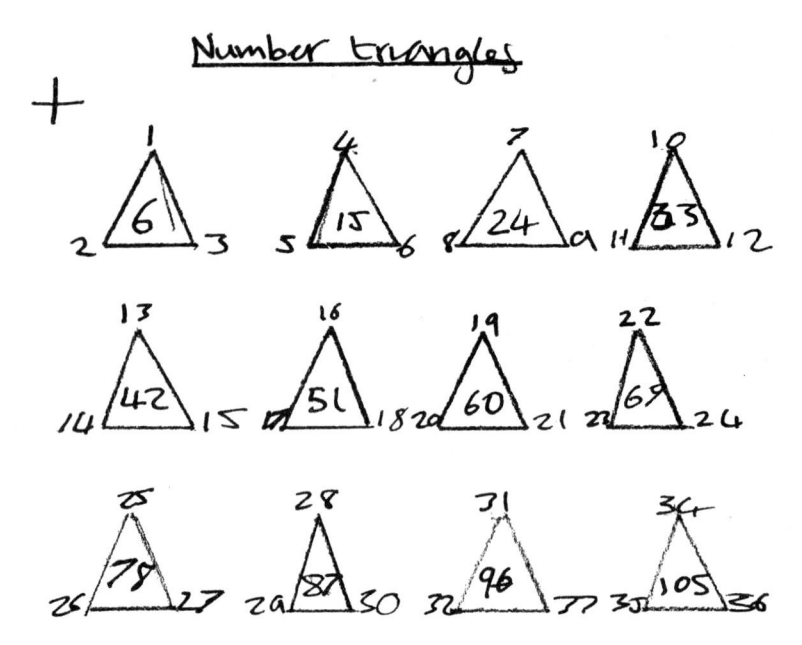

△ 1, 2/6\3
△ 4, 5/15\6
△ 7, 8/24\9
△ 10, 11/33\12

△ 13, 14/42\15
△ 16, 17/51\18
△ 19, 20/60\21
△ 22, 23/69\24

△ 25, 26/78\27
△ 28, 29/87\30
△ 31, 32/96\33
△ 34, 35/105\36

Figure 11 Danny's number triangles

6.34 Lisa's work shows one pupil-defined task emerging out of Adrienne's open-ended task. Danny was another member of the class who investigated number triangles; his work, part of which is shown in Figure 11, provided another distinctly different pupil-defined task. Danny completed 28 triangles in this series, and then went on to try multiplying the same set of triples.

6.35 Sitting next to Lisa, Joanne decided to try number triangles which involved multiplication as well as addition. On the page she tried both multiplication and addition. Her work, shown in Figure 12, eventually covered 49 separate calculations. This appears to lack the systematic character of Lisa's work but this does not mean that a task cannot be negotiated from it. There are many possibilities to build on:

- Which triangles have the biggest, or the smallest, results?
- Some results differ by only one. Why is that?
- If you put the same three numbers at different corners of the triangle, will you get the same result?
- When you multiply and add the same three numbers you get different answers. Is this always true? Are there three numbers which give the same result whether multiplied or added?

6.36 The last challenge was taken up by Joanne. She tried out possibilities and quickly discovered that the numbers she needed were small; the smaller she made them the closer the two results became. Eventually she found the numbers she needed: 1, 2 and 3. Shortly after this, she started to include zeros in the calculations. Then she told

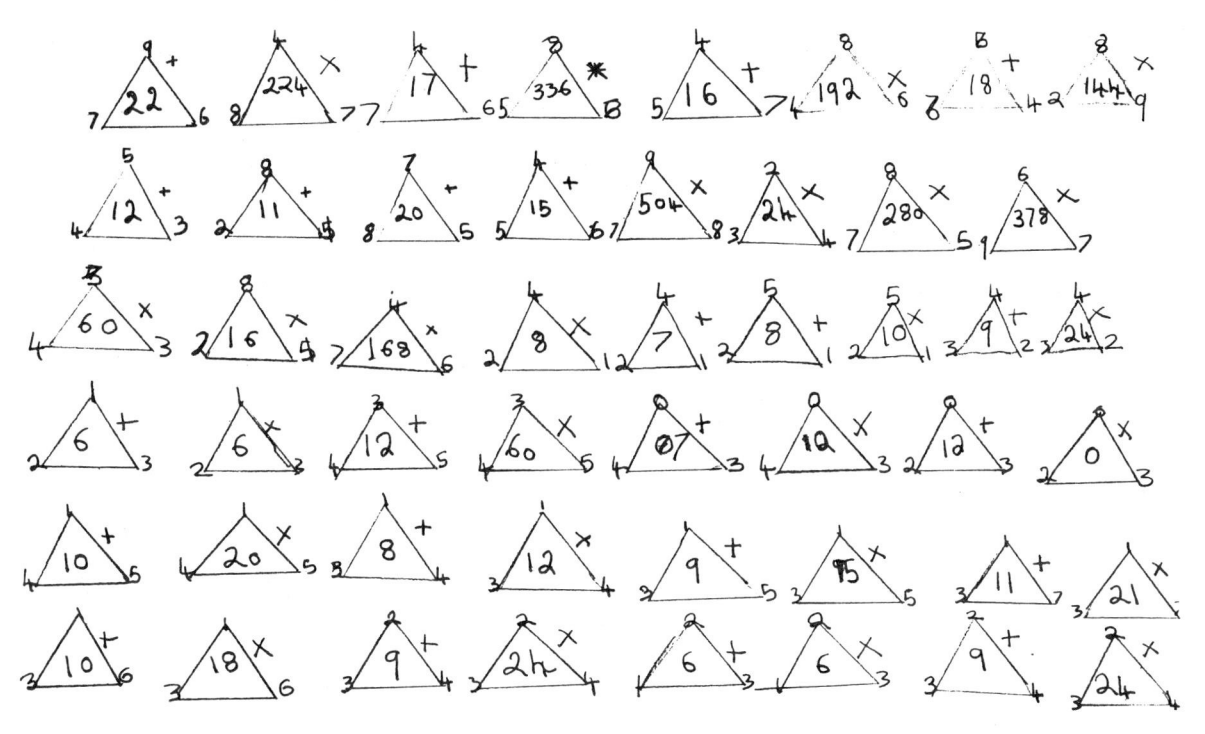

Figure 12 Joanne's number triangles

Adrienne she had discovered that whenever there was a zero in the three numbers and she multiplied them using a calculator, the answer was always zero. But this didn't happen when she added.

6.37 In the episode involving Shane working with the series of equilateral triangles we saw the process of negotiating a task. Adrienne felt that Shane and Ian's initial choice of task was not challenging enough and decided to suggest a new problem. They started with the problem: How many triangles are in each row of the figure, and what is the rule for this series? They quickly saw that this produced the series 1, 3, 5, 7, 9, and so on. In the programme you saw Adrienne negotiating a new challenge with Shane: How many triangles are in the figure as a whole, and how does this number grow as we add successive rows to it?

'How many triangles altogether?'

6.38 Diversification in this lesson derives from the choice the pupils have in the lines of enquiry they pursue. At the end of Section 5, I criticized the notion of matching tasks to pupils as simply raising or lowering the difficulty level. We can see in Adrienne's work another respect in which this is a limited view. In this lesson, the tasks are created by these pupils and their teachers jointly. The process of creating the task is an essential part of the pupils' active learning. The matching of task and pupil is not predefined, but developed collaboratively.

TEACHER–PUPIL DIALOGUE

6.39   I asked you to focus on the dialogue between teacher and pupils in the baked bean tin and triangle activities. In Section 5, I discussed the consequences for talk in the classroom when the teacher defines the lesson script. In these two lessons the situation is different. To extend the theatrical analogy, Adrienne and Barbara have written the outline synopsis for these lessons, but the script is negotiated with the pupils. The resulting dialogue is rather different in character from the examples we considered in Section 5. We can think of it in terms of two broad functions: interpretation and intervention.

Interpretation

6.40   There is no shortage of questions from Barbara and Adrienne, but in these dialogues, the teachers do not know all the answers in advance. Questions are not there to get children to complete blank slots in the lesson script. They are there to get the children to tell their teacher what their script is. Barbara's dialogue with both Matthew and Mark began with asking them to explain what they were doing, so she could interpret the way they have chosen to approach the task. Adrienne's dialogue with Lisa was also predominantly interpretive. Adrienne sought Lisa's own interpretation of her work. She was also able to discover patterns in Lisa's work that Lisa herself had not yet noticed.

6.41   What might this interpretive dialogue achieve? First of all, in these episodes, the teacher provides a genuine audience for pupils, giving them a reason to make their thinking explicit. This helps to establish a shared understanding about the task on which further dialogue can be based. It also helps the children to understand the problem they are working on by forcing them to 'verbalize' their thinking. When we have to tell someone else what we understand, it can help us to see the gaps in our thinking, and develop a firmer understanding. In Section 7 I shall look further at the role of verbalization. Second, the pupils' efforts are given serious attention and value. Third, the interpretation provides a basis for further support for the pupils' learning.

Intervention

6.42   Barbara's dialogue with Mark and Matthew involves an intervention in the tasks that they have set themselves. In Matthew's case she needed to help him to see a mistake he had made. In Mark's case she needed to help him move to the next stage of his task. In both cases, there was a process of guided discovery. Rather than crudely telling Matthew he was wrong, she helped him to see the mistake. Rather than telling Mark how to improve on his method of finding the number of tins in a stack from the number of layers, she pointed out the limitations of the method and steered him towards a more efficient solution. In both cases, the pupils were given a reason to move forward that came from the task itself. The problem, not the teacher, provides the motive to continue to work.

6.43   In Adrienne's lesson, we saw another kind of intervention with Shane: the negotiation of a new task. Perhaps the most significant feature of this dialogue was Shane saying: 'So what are you trying to say, Miss?'. He realized that he was not clear what the new problem was, and he was willing to make this clear to Adrienne. In Section 5, I discussed the difficulties pupils face in saying they do not understand. Encouraging an environment in which children have the confidence to take such action is important. Pupils need to know that they will gain, not lose, by making their uncertainty clear. Adrienne used a variety of strategies to clarify the new problem. First she talked it through, then she got Shane to build the first two or three elements in the sequence, and discussed those. Not shown in the film was the third stage, when she sat down and demonstrated the task herself.

Dialogue on paper

6.44   In her written comments on pupils' work Barbara continued the dialogue. Here is a selection of her comments on Matthew and Mark's work from a series of lessons on baked bean tins. We can see a mix of interpretation and intervention here. There are also comments which are evaluative: they tell the pupil how he has done. These are all task-related and specific.

> *Comments to Matthew:*
>
> Well done for predicting for eight levels. Can you write about how you did it? Could you work out how many tins would be in 20 levels?
>
> Have you thought about stacking your tins differently?
>
> *Comments to Mark:*
>
> Can you use your 'rule' to work out how many tins in 50 layers?
>
> This is really interesting. How have you worked out what to multiply by?
>
> Clearly expressed.
>
> Can you write your rule on page 7 in a shorter way?

LEARNING SUPPORT IN A DIVERSE CLASSROOM

6.45   In the Maxbox lesson I asked you to concentrate on the role of learning support teacher, Barbara Ritchie, and how the lesson organization fosters collaboration between pupils. We can see both of these as forms of support for pupils' learning. You will recall from Section 3 that the effectiveness of a learning support teacher depends on

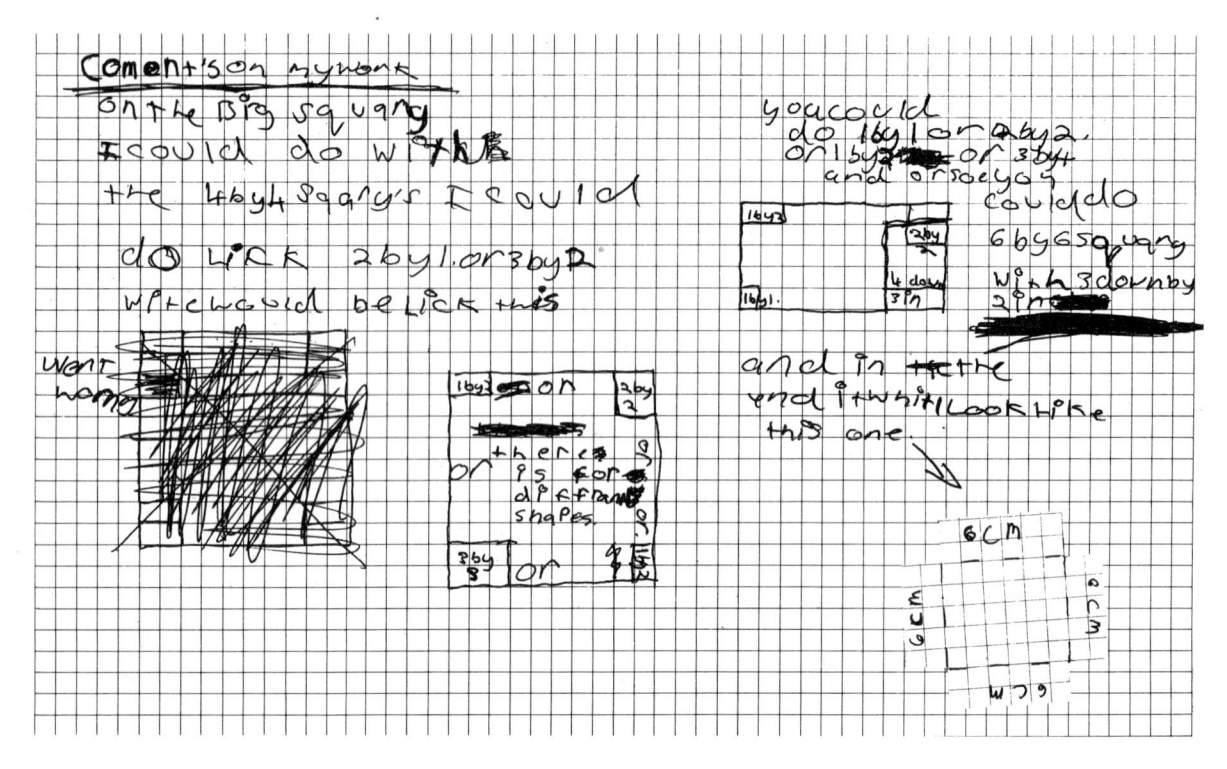

Figure 13   Brian's maxbox homework

the organization of lessons. In this lesson, Barbara Ritchie was as actively involved as Barbara Miller. Their roles were almost interchangeable. Collaboration is the subject of Section 7, so I shall not say too much about it here. But it is worth pointing out how the diversification of learning in this lesson led to pupils being resources for each other's learning. Note that pupils are producing individual pieces of work, but this does not prevent them from collaborating in various ways.

6.46   The first pupils you saw in the Maxbox lesson were Brian and Chris. To see how collaboration supported their learning, we need to begin with what each pupil was trying to achieve, and the difficulties they faced. Brian's main challenge was drawing a net on paper so that it would fold into an open box when it was cut out. His homework before the lesson was filmed (shown in Figure 13) illustrates this. Chris did not have this problem, but he was not clear about what the volume of the box meant. He explained to Barbara Ritchie how he had calculated the volume of a 6 × 6 × 2 cm box, drawn on graph paper marked in 0.5 cm squares. He added up all the 'little squares' on the base, then divided by 2. The answer was 72, since there were 144 0.5 cm squares marked on the base. This also happens to be the correct value of the volume. He had the 'right answer' but his method showed that this answer had nothing to do with volume. Barbara Ritchie asked Chris to work practically with centicubes (1 cm plastic cubes that fix together) so he could get a sense of what volume means.

6.47 By the time Chris had nearly completed this, Brian was drawing the net for a 6 × 6 × 2 cm box. Barbara Ritchie then asked Chris to share his work with Brian. This had two effects. First it required Chris to explain what he had done. Here is another way in which pupils can be encouraged to be explicit about their thinking. Second, Brian benefited directly from Chris's explanation. This is another way in which, in the lesson, the teachers were not the sole possessors of 'the answers'. That Brian understood Chris's reasoning is evident in how he recorded the result:

Area was 6 by 6 and that = 36

the volom was 2 layers of 36

36 × 2 = 72

6.48 The benefit of collaboration in this example derived from the fact that Chris and Brian were working at different levels in the activity. Temporarily, Chris acted as teacher for Brian, whose thinking was supported and extended by Chris's explanation, and Brian provided an audience for Chris, giving him a reason to make his thinking explicit. Later, Brian accurately drew, cut out and calculated the volume of two more boxes. Chris went on to calculate correctly the volume of a box with sides of 0.5 cm – something for which he could not rely on the centicubes.

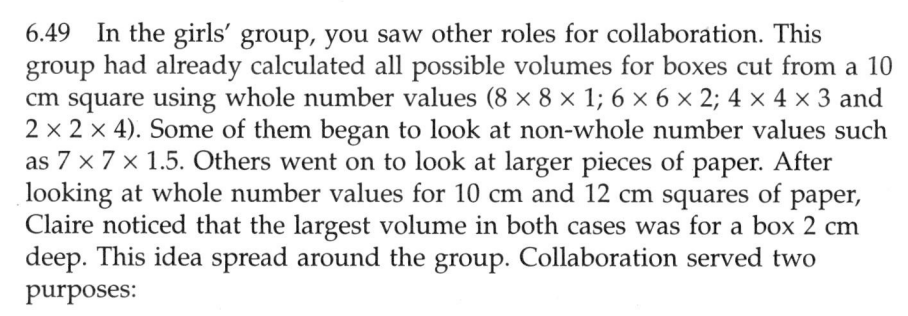

'One of these matches four of them small ones'

6.49 In the girls' group, you saw other roles for collaboration. This group had already calculated all possible volumes for boxes cut from a 10 cm square using whole number values (8 × 8 × 1; 6 × 6 × 2; 4 × 4 × 3 and 2 × 2 × 4). Some of them began to look at non-whole number values such as 7 × 7 × 1.5. Others went on to look at larger pieces of paper. After looking at whole number values for 10 cm and 12 cm squares of paper, Claire noticed that the largest volume in both cases was for a box 2 cm deep. This idea spread around the group. Collaboration served two purposes:

(a) On Barbara Miller's suggestion, the routine calculating was shared out. Some members of the group shifted from an individual to a shared task.

(b) Ideas came into conflict. Lyndsey was one of the group who had investigated non-whole number values with the 10 cm square of paper. She pointed out that Claire's theory didn't seem to work, since a depth for the box of 1.5 cm gave a larger volume than a depth of 2 cm. Claire quickly replied that she wasn't talking about halves. She was not going to give up her theory that easily! But she had to abandon it when she got to a 16 cm square of paper. In Section 7, I shall say more about the role of conflicting ideas.

'Do you think she might be right if we only use whole numbers?'

In this case Lyndsey's intervention served to refine Claire's theory. Perhaps if Claire had been more tentative and willing to consider alternatives, this could have been a more powerful learning opportunity. Being tentative and exploratory in collaborative settings is an issue I shall return to in the next section.

'Where are your three ways, Shane?'

6.50 In the final part of the programme, with the water game activity, you saw one more way in which collaboration can support learning. The challenge to the class as a whole was to find all possible arrangements of the triangles. Children worked mainly on an individual basis towards this joint project, which continued into further lessons. The shared project provided important motivation for a wide range of responses.

SUMMARY

6.51 Teaching that requires all children in a class to do the same task is a source of learning difficulty for some children: the lesson is unlikely to be appropriate for all children; children are more likely to be passive participants in such lessons; there is considerable potential for misunderstanding; the opportunities for pupils to signal misunderstanding are limited. The effects of being adrift from lessons accumulate over time.

6.52 To overcome these problems, some teachers have moved to individualized learning. It has been noted that this strategy reduces the adverse effects of homogeneous teaching, and gives an active role to learning support teachers. But it also places heavy demands on the quality of materials and can reduce contact between teacher and pupils. Although pupils work on a variety of tasks in one lesson they have limited chances to shape their tasks themselves. Pupils also miss opportunities to use each other as resources.

6.53 An alternative approach to lesson and task organization is through the provision of relatively open-ended tasks which allow a wide range of response from pupils, require decisions from pupils as to how they will tackle them, and enable the teacher to negotiate the precise task with pupils.

6.54 The mathematics tasks we have examined make minimal demands on reading skills and memory, give pupils opportunities to respond in a range of ways – through practical activities, talk and writing – and allow pupils to use their skills for a purpose to which they are committed.

6.55 Diversification encourages pupils to be active learners in that they are encouraged to make decisions about how to define and approach the task, formulate their own ideas, and communicate these ideas to others.

6.56 Diversification helps to sustain a dialogue between teacher and pupils in which the teacher bases intervention on interpretation.

6.57 Diversification helps pupils to use each other as resources by being teachers to each other, being audiences for each other, sharing out routine work, bringing ideas into conflict, and providing the motivation of a shared project.

7 COLLABORATIVE LEARNING

7.1 We have already seen instances of children learning together in groups, working to some degree independently of their teacher. In this section I am going to examine collaborative learning more systematically, and explore its potential to support the learning of pupils who experience difficulties, especially in diverse groups. I shall begin with a brief survey of the many and various arguments for collaborative learning that have been advanced, and some of the rather different conceptions of collaborative learning associated with them. Then I shall investigate the potential of collaborative learning in groups that include children who have been Statemented as having moderate learning difficulties. I shall do this through a case study of a part-time integration scheme involving a special school and a junior school, which is the subject of Cassette Programme 2. Then I shall look at how teachers have tried to create classroom environments which foster collaboration. The section ends with TV Programme 4. Make sure you read up to Activity 17 before watching the programme.

WHAT IS COLLABORATION FOR?

7.2 Collaborative learning covers an enormous range of classroom practices, and these practices are seen by different teachers and writers in education as means to a wide range of goals, some of which conflict with each other. The versions of collaborative learning which I shall discuss in some detail later in this section, and the educational purposes they are intended to achieve, are distinctly different from some other versions and their educational purposes.

Peer tutoring

7.3 One version of collaborative learning that acquired currency in special education in this country during the 1980s is 'peer tutoring'. Peer tutoring involves children acting as teachers to other children. It has been widely advocated as a means to increase the achievement of children who are tutored (tutees) as well as those who act as tutors, and it has been the subject of a great deal of research in which children who experience difficulties in learning act as tutors and tutees. It is not a new development, and this is recognized by many of its proponents. Throughout educational history, pupils have been used in various ways as aides to teachers. In the late eighteenth and early nineteenth century, peer tutoring, under the name of the 'monitorial system', devised and developed by Andrew Bell and Joseph Lancaster, became widely practised in England.

7.4   Peer tutoring has been used for many purposes and with many different groups of children. In most, though not all cases, when it has been used with children with learning difficulties it has been to improve basic skills in reading, writing, spelling and number work. And in most, but not all cases, the tutors have been children who are older, or have higher attainments, than the tutees. A good example of how peer tutoring has been used is contained in a study by Kevin Wheldall and Paul Mettem (1985). They taught 16-year-old children in the remedial stream of a comprehensive school to teach 12-year-old children in the same stream of the same school. The tutoring was aimed at improving the reading of the younger children, and tutors were taught to teach them using a technique called 'pause, prompt and praise'. The aim of this technique is to encourage children to correct themselves as they read, to correct them when they do not correct themselves, and to encourage the child by offering frequent praise for success. The tutor is taught to wait for five seconds after a reading error, or until the end of a sentence, to allow the tutee to self-correct. If the child has not corrected the error herself, the tutor is then expected to provide clues, and only then to tell the child the word. The tutor is also asked to praise the tutee frequently for correct reading. In this study the tutees made six months of progress in reading accuracy and comprehension, measured by a reading test, over its two month course. Tutees with similar abilities who were taught by untrained tutors, and children with similar abilities who just spent the same time in silent reading made less progress.

7.5   This study is similar to other examples of peer tutoring in a number of respects:

(a) It is tightly organized and prescribed, taking a specific timetable slot, using a specific technique, and often seen as a supplement to the rest of the curriculum. In a guide to peer tutoring, Keith Topping (1988) says that:

> Tutoring is usually characterized by careful matching of tutor and tutee, specification of frequent and regular contact times, training in some form of tutoring technique including correction procedures, clear specification of curriculum content and possibly materials, a system for monitoring and supervision, and possibly some form of evaluation.

(Topping, 1988, p. 1)

(b) It uses tutors who are expected to act in an authoritative capacity. The tutors are the experts who have the right to define behaviour from the tutee as acceptable or unacceptable, and they are selected to be more competent than the tutee. This does not mean that they will always be older. In a lot of cases children of the same age have been paired as tutors and tutees. Topping recommends that the tutor's attainment should be two years ahead of the tutee, otherwise,

> if a minimal differential in ability is not maintained, and the tutor's abilities approximate to those of the tutee, then very

little gain in attainment can be expected from the tutees, except those resulting from increased time on task.

(Topping, 1988, p. 32)

(c) The form that the teaching takes is highly controlled. The tutee has only limited opportunities to define and shape the task. In Wheldall and Mettem's study, the objective was accurate reading, and the study does not allow for, or refer to, other reading activities, such as discussing the meaning of the text.

(d) The tutees made measurable progress in reading by comparison with children who did not receive tuition from trained tutors. Most, but not all, reports of carefully designed peer tutoring show increases in tutees' ability in the skill being taught. Tutors also make progress. Keith Topping concludes:

> Gains for tutors as well as tutees are widely reported, involving increased attainment in the subject area of tutoring and in positive attitudes to each other and to the subject area ... No doubter can now rationally oppose peer tutoring on the grounds that it is not effective.

(Topping, 1988, p. 92)

7.6 Now the choice we make of an educational method depends on many criteria and, sometimes, we are only partially aware of those criteria. Thus most of us, whether involved professionally in education or not, react against some educational practices with every fibre of our being, although it is not always easy to say exactly what precepts and values are offended. Peer tutoring can certainly claim to be effective in many cases, if by this we mean 'achieving measurable results in specific basic skills over a defined time span, by comparison with children who were not tutored'. But in assessing the claims of any advocate of a particular approach, including all those mentioned in this course, it is wise to ask some questions.

7.7 First, compared to what is the method effective? In many research reports on the learning outcomes of teaching methods, effectiveness is measured by comparison with the absence of the method, rather than by comparison to another, completely different approach. In others, methods are directly compared against each other. In weighing such evidence with a view to using the method in question in a school, the rational question to ask is whether it is likely that the method will be effective by comparison with what already happens in the school. Unfortunately it is rarely possible for research reports to anticipate the need for such comparisons, and so claims for effectiveness in research studies can seldom be used on their own to take a decision on whether or not to adopt the method. Judgement and locally collected information inevitably enter into the decision.

7.8 Second, would the method be the same method, with the same effects, if it was put into practice in another setting? There is always a critical gap between the conditions in which a research study on an educational method is conducted, and the conditions under which the method concerned is put into practice. Many factors change: the school, the pupils, the teachers, the particular way in which the ideas are put into effect, and the modifications forced on those involved by practicalities and personal preferences. All these limit the relevance of research findings and demand the exercise of informed judgement. They do not, though, make research findings useless.

7.9   Third, other than the effects on which the claim for effectiveness is based, what other effects might the method have? Peer tutoring fosters an authority relationship, temporary at least, between tutor and tutee, and places the tutee as a relatively dependent learner, with limited opportunities to challenge and change the basis on which she is taught, or to bring her existing understanding to bear. In effect, peer tutoring reproduces the asymmetrical relationship between teacher and pupil which I discussed in Section 5. It may also define, for both tutor and tutee, the nature of educational interaction between peers in a particular way. It may encourage them to see the roles they can fulfil in collaborative settings as limited to 'the teacher' and 'the taught'. Later in this section, I shall describe and illustrate other kinds of roles for learners in collaborative settings. These effects need to be assessed as well as the measured gain in skill.

7.10   So practices which go under the title 'collaborative learning', a term which suggests a move away from lessons in which teachers are all-powerful, may turn out on closer inspection not to support this move. (This is not to imply that all practices called 'peer tutoring' involve hierarchical relationships between tutor and tutee.) In assessing any practice, including collaborative learning, we need to ask what goals the practice supports and whether we concur with them.

Democracy or economic efficiency?

7.11   In the USA there has been an enormous amount of interest in collaborative learning since the early 1970s. Like peer tutoring, the larger part of this work has been concerned with the development of techniques in which pupils' learning has remained under close direction by the teacher. A particular concern has been to use collaboration to provide a 'motivational structure' which will encourage children to learn the material set for them by the teacher. Two examples of commonly used techniques will help to make this clear. One is known as Teams–Games–Tournaments (TGT) (DeVries and Slavin, 1978). The class is divided into mixed-ability teams, who are all given worksheets to learn. The collective aim of the team is to help each other learn this material, and prepare for the 'tournament'. In this test of what they have learned, children are regrouped in threes, of similar attainment, who compete against each other as representatives of their teams. Teams are ranked and rewarded according to their joint performance. The aim of the method is to give each individual the added incentive to perform well for the good of the team.

7.12 Another teacher-directed technique for collaboration is the jigsaw method (Aronson, 1978). In this approach, the class is split into 'home groups', whose task is to learn a particular topic. The topic is then broken down into a number of different subtopics, and each one of these is assigned to an 'expert group'. Every child becomes a member of one expert group, so that every home group has its expert in each subtopic. For example, a project about rain forests might have expert groups on global warming, animals and plants, exploitation of natural resources, indigenous peoples, etc. The expert groups learn their subtopics, and then return to their home group so the group as a whole can complete their work on the topic. In the original American version, there follows a test on the topic, in which children are ranked and rewarded as individuals. Again the method is designed to ensure that every child has an incentive to learn the expert material, because the performance of every other child in the home group depends on it. Jigsaw has been taken up in this country, but in rather different ways, for competitive testing of groups is not an essential element of the method. Primary teachers have found jigsaw a useful way to organize extended projects by assigning children specialist roles.

7.13 In the original form of these methods, collaboration serves as a means by which children can see reasons to compete against each other, and depend on each other for success. The ideology behind such methods is well captured by the following slogan from an American text on cooperative learning: 'Cooperation is basic to all human interaction and provides the context for competition and individualization. Cooperation is the forest; competition and individualization are but trees' (Johnson and Johnson, 1975, p. 22). Johnson and Johnson, major proponents of collaborative learning in the USA, are very clear about what kind of pupils they wish schools to produce:

> Students should be taught the values, habits, knowledge, attitudes, and skills needed to fill specific adult roles and to live a fulfilling, satisfying life in a complex, democratic industrial society. They should develop the capacity for 'role-responsibility' (i.e., the capacity to live up to general expectations of appropriate role behaviour, such as promptness and cleanliness) and 'role readiness' (i.e., the ability to meet the demands of many organizational settings with the proper cooperation); they should commit themselves to occupational roles, become 'self-actualizing' (i.e., develop their personal potentials, resources, and abilities and utilize them in living a fulfilling life), have enough personal flexibility to live in a rapidly changing world, and enjoy healthy physical and psychological development.
> (Johnson and Johnson, 1975, p. 29)

7.14 You might like to consider how far you agree with this list of aims. In doing so you might think about what is not in the list, as well as what is in. My personal list of aims for participants in an industrial democracy would include independence of thought and the ability to criticize and act against unjust and irrational authority. What would yours include?

7.15 It has been argued that a similar ideology is at work behind some of the official encouragement to use collaborative learning methods in British education. Cooperation in small groups was widely promoted in developments in the 14–16 curriculum during the 1980s, in the development of prevocational education and in courses on Personal and Social Education (PSE), aimed particularly at lower-attaining young people at secondary school and college. I shall not go into detail about these courses, since you will be examining them in Unit 13. Douglas Barnes (1988) has scrutinized the aims of fostering cooperation in the classroom in these courses:

> There is strong evidence ... that employers want something different from what schools have previously provided, and it seems likely that this is because extensive changes are expected in patterns of work. Why should employers value awareness of others' perspectives, the ability to work together, effective communication, the ability to take responsibility, when in the past the most valued characteristics have been accuracy, obedience and punctuality? Three hesitant answers can be offered. It has been suggested that in future a larger proportion of the population will be employed in service industries, in which the need to please the client face-to-face is of central importance ... Moreover, for many years both industrial and commercial concerns have been willing to send their managers on expensive, privately run courses, which use group problem-solving methods to change their attitudes and skills in working and communicating with others. Although industry and commerce are built on competition, in the running of their concerns they need to employ people who can collaborate and show sensitivity to others' needs. Moreover, some of the most economically successful producers, both in Europe and in the Far East, base their success on rapid response to changes in market demand: to change products so rapidly requires not only design and technical resources, but attitudes and flexibility in the workforce that will make radical changes possible without prolonged negotiation with unions ... It is ironical if, because of these projected changes in work patterns, industry is making 'liberal' proposals for collaborative practices in secondary schools, since in preparing students for examinations schools can hardly avoid promulgating the values of individualism and competition.
>
> (Barnes, 1988, pp. 51–2)

7.16 Now my aim here is not to persuade you of the duplicity and malign cunning of British employers, nor that schools should not be concerned with helping young people to get and hold down jobs. It is simply to persuade you of the need to question what is achieved by educational practices, and whose interests are supported by their development. And there is no guaranteed connection between the aims of a teaching method and its outcomes. Whether collaboration in the classroom does produce the flexible person-centred workforce that Barnes suggests that employers want is a question yet to be answered. In fact, collaboration has also been argued to be an essential preparation for critical autonomous participants in a democratic society. This case is put, for example, by Helen Cowie and Jean Ruddock (1990):

> The skills which are fundamental to group work, such as the ability to acknowledge the range of perspectives which may be brought to bear on an issue, form the basis of democracy (Bridges, 1979). At a time when there are many pressures from minority groups within our society for rights and justice, there is a growing feeling in some quarters that it is the responsibility of schools to give their pupils, regardless of gender, social class or ethnic background, the confidence and the ability to make their voices heard within their own community and in society at large.
>
> (Cowie and Ruddock, 1990, p. 236)

HOW CAN COLLABORATION SUPPORT LEARNING?

7.17 So far I have looked at what classroom collaboration might achieve in the long term. Now I want to turn to the more detailed learning process that can take place in collaborative groups. I shall be concerned here with examples of collaboration in which the pupils are able to be independent, active learners. What exactly might collaborative learning have to offer to children, over and above what they could gain from a more teacher-directed approach?

7.18 When I looked at the way pupils supported each other in Barbara Miller's maths lessons, I pointed to four important processes:

- making thinking explicit;
- children who understand something supporting children who understand less;
- conflicts of ideas;
- being tentative and exploring alternatives.

I shall now say a little more about each of these processes.

Making thinking explicit

7.19 In groups, pupils provide a ready-made audience for each other, which gives them a reason to say out loud what they are thinking. Making our thinking explicit in this way can be a powerful learning device. It bears some similarities to the power of writing as a tool for learning. The idea that writing consists of two stages – getting the ideas straight and then putting them on paper – is a misconception. I rarely know fully what I am trying to say until I try to write it down, and then

I often discover something wrong with it and have to rewrite it. E. M. Forster remarked: 'How can I know what I think till I see what I say?'. In the right circumstances, collaborative learning groups offer children many opportunities to 'see what they say' and so know what they think. Verbalization, as psychologists know it, has been the subject of research which has measured its effects on learning. For example, Ben Fletcher (1985) got Year 5–7 children to try to solve a problem based on a computer game. In this game, the children had to imagine that the Earth was under attack by aliens and they were in charge of a spaceship in which people would escape from the Earth. But they have to take guns as well to shoot down alien ships. The computer gave them targets for the number of passengers to take and the number of alien spaceships they must shoot down. At each move children had to input to the computer the size of spaceship and the number of guns they thought they would need. The computer knows the relationships between these inputs and the targets it sets, and after each move tells the children the number of passengers they can take and the number of alien spaceships shot down, given the inputs they have just made for that move. The children's task is to reach the target in as few moves as possible. The faster they can deduce the relationships the computer knows, the faster they can reach the target. Fletcher got children to play the game on their own and in pairs. On their own, children were told either to play without talking, or they were encouraged to talk through the reasons for their decisions as they went along. In pairs, they had to explain their reasons to each other and reach a consensus before telling the computer their next guess. Fletcher found that the silent individuals performed worst, and in general the pairs were most effective in reaching the target. But in one particularly difficult version of the task, the pairs did worse than the individuals who verbalized their reasons. He suggests that this may be because the difficulty of the task made it hard for pairs to reach a consensus.

7.20 This experimental evidence supports the evidence of common sense: getting children to make their ideas explicit can assist problem-solving. When children work on their own they do not often talk through their ideas; in our society this practice is strongly deprecated. In a group, there are many more reasons to make ideas explicit. Indeed, if there is a joint task to be achieved, and consensus is required, there is little option but to explain your thinking. However, we have seen from Fletcher's study that if the task is too difficult, and produces disagreements that the members of the group have no way to resolve, collaboration may not help. Clearly this depends on what the group is expected to do. If consensus is not required, then the group might reasonably conclude that they cannot make progress productively.

Supporting ideas

7.21 We have seen circumstances in which children act as tutors to each other, but there are also less obvious and less formalized ways in which children in mixed-ability groups can support each others' learning. You saw one such example in the case of Brian and Chris in TV3. One of the important theoretical bases for collaborative learning is the work of the Russian developmental psychologist, L. S. Vygotsky, whose ideas, developed in the 1920s and 1930s, have come to play an increasingly significant role in educational thinking in the UK since the early 1980s. Vygotsky's work provides a framework within which we can think about some features of classroom collaboration. Vygotsky stressed the social nature of development, arguing that children develop through and as a result of social interaction. He drew a distinction between what a child could do individually and what the same child could do with social support. He argued that 'the only "good learning" is that which is in advance of development' (Vygotsky, 1978, p. 89). What a child could do as part of a social activity, but not do alone, Vygotsky referred to as 'the zone of proximal development': this is 'the distance between the actual developmental level as determined by independent problem solving and the level of potential development as determined through problem solving under adult guidance or in collaboration with more capable peers' (Vygotsky, 1978, p. 86). For Vygotsky important learning happened in this area: it was through social support that children learned new skills, which they could then take on as individuals.

7.22 The American psychologist Jerome Bruner has been a powerful advocate of Vygotskian thinking in education. He chose the term 'scaffolding' to refer to the ways in which children gained social support for their learning in the 'zone of proximal development':

> If the child is enabled to advance by being under the tutelage of an adult or a more competent peer, then the tutor or the aiding peer serves the learner as a vicarious form of consciousness until such a time as the learner is able to master his own action through his own consciousness and control. When the child achieves that conscious control over the new function or conceptual system, it is then that he is able to use it as a tool. Up to that point, the tutor in effect performs the critical function of 'scaffolding' the learning task to make it possible for the child, in Vygotsky's word, to internalize external knowledge and convert it into a tool for conscious control.
>
> (Bruner, 1985, pp. 24–5)

We shall shortly see some examples of the way in which scaffolding of learning can take place in mixed-ability groups with children identified as having moderate learning difficulties.

Ideas in conflict

7.23 In TV3 you saw how, in the girls' group in the Maxbox lesson, there was a conflict between two theories of what determined the maximum volume of the box. Conflict between ideas is another important theoretical basis for collaborative learning and has been the subject of a great deal of experimental work in developmental psychology, as well as classroom based work. The basic premise is not complicated: having someone with you who proposes a different solution to a problem encourages you to see that there are other viewpoints, to think about alternatives, and to reassess your own solution. The point here is not that children face a correct solution and realize the error they have made, although that can happen. Conflict between ideas can lead to progress whether or not either solution is correct; and in many tasks there is in any case no 'correct' solution at all.

7.24 The most substantial body of research in this area is that produced by Doise, Mugny and Perret-Clermont, psychologists at the University of Geneva (Doise and Mugny, 1984). In many studies they have shown that children working in pairs to solve a range of problems perform better than children working as individuals. For example, one task they used involves the 'conservation of length'. Given two rods of equal length laid side by side so that their ends coincide, young children aged 5 or 6 will usually agree that they are the same length. But displace one so that they remain parallel but their ends no longer coincide, and many children this age will insist that they are no longer the same length. Children in this situation tend to attend to one end or the other, but find it difficult to take the location of both ends into account simultaneously. Doise and Mugny (1984) found that by putting pairs of children together to work at this task, conflict between their interpretations would often arise, with the two children claiming that different rods were longer. This conflict, in this case between two wrong answers, was often enough to get the children to improve on their solutions: 'having to keep one's own point of view in mind while being obliged to take into account another incompatible perspective can lead to progress' (Doise, 1990, p. 51). A study by Paul Light and Martin Glachan (1985) suggests that in more complicated problem-solving tasks, the level of debate between conflicting ideas in the group is important to the progress made. In this study, children worked in pairs at a computer version of the game 'Mastermind'. In this game, Year 3–4 children had to discover a hidden sequence of digits by making a series of guesses. After each guess, the computer told the children how many digits they had correct, and how many were in the right place in the sequence. Pairs solved the problems faster than individuals, and pairs who expressed their arguments and reasons for guesses and debated them a lot solved the problems faster than pairs that did not. Light and Glachan conclude:

> Productive interactions were marked by the fact that the two children remained focused on the particular problem and resolved their disagreement through argument. It was relatively unimportant whether, in the particular case, the agreed outcome was the 'correct' one or not. Amongst the low argument/low progress subgroup, disagreements generally resulted in attempts by one or both of the children to defend or assert their 'status'. In such cases children would raise their voices, claim simply to *know* what was right or just attempt to press ahead despite their partner's protests. In the longer term either one partner established dominance over the other or rules such as turn-taking were invoked by the children to defuse the situation.
>
> (Light and Glachan, 1985, p. 223)

7.25 Here authority and compliance – asymmetry of power between two children – are the enemies of learning. Doise has found that the same 'dynamic of compliance' can prevent the productive use of conflict:

> A highly asymmetric interaction between a subject who unhesitatingly adopted the correct solution and another who was not yet able to find it, very rarely ended in progress for the latter. The more advanced subject, being more confident, simply imposed his solution without even considering the solution offered by the other, and there was no real confrontation of views.
>
> (Doise, 1990, p. 52)

Exploratory thinking

7.26 If the dynamic of compliance depends on asserting your position dogmatically, then it would be reasonable to argue that progress in collaborative groups would be fostered by talk that was tentative and exploratory in nature. In Reader 1, Chapter 4 we saw some examples of children discussing scientific ideas in this way; and in TV3 you may remember Claire's rather definitive assertion of her solution to the Maxbox problem. Douglas Barnes (1976), who has been a key figure in the development of collaborative learning methods in the UK, argues that exploratory speculative talk is a vital part of learning.

LEARNING TOGETHER IN PRACTICE

Cassette programme 2

7.27 Let's now see how these various possibilities for collaborative learning work out in practice. In the autumn of 1990, together with staff working in two schools in Dudley, in the West Midlands, and one of the LEA's advisory teachers, we established a curriculum project that would allow us to explore what collaboration could offer when groups are very diverse in nature. The project involved a class from Sutton School, a special school for children identified as having moderate learning difficulties, working together with a class from Russells Hall School, a primary school. We visited the project on a number of occasions during the term to talk to the teachers and the pupils about what was happening, and to record learning in progress. The results of this work have been put onto Cassette programme 2, and you will shortly be listening to this. First, Chris Morris, the advisory teacher who worked on the project, introduces it.

Activity 14 Organizing a collaborative project

Now read 'Opening Doors: learning history through talk' by Chris Morris (Reader 1, Chapter 2). This chapter sets out the main stages of the project and describes the key learning experiences for the children. Note how the project was organized, and the kinds of tasks children were presented with.

7.28 Part-time integration schemes between special schools for children with moderate learning difficulties and ordinary schools are now quite common, although they tend to be small scale (Jowett, Hegarty and Moses, 1988). There has been little systematic research on these schemes. My own observations suggest that in some of them children from special schools join a mainstream class but they do not share a common curriculum. Sometimes, children from a special school simply do work set by their special school teacher in the mainstream classroom. It is argued that this has 'social benefits' for the integrating children. However, since the part-time classmates have few reasons to talk to each other, socializing can be an uphill struggle. In discussing different forms of integration, the Warnock Report (DES, 1978) distinguished between locational, social and functional integration. Locational integration means having the two groups in the same place but that's all. Social integration means the two groups having chances to be together informally at times such as breaks. Functional integration refers to the children learning together in the classroom. The report saw these as 'progressive stages of association' (p. 100). Yet learning together provides probably the most important reason for children to socialize in and out of lessons. The idea that a child should progress from social to functional integration seems rather odd. In this project, the two groups of children had reasons to work together and so got to know each other.

Activity 15   All sorts of ideas: collaborative learning in practice

Now listen to Cassette programme 2. At various points I will ask you to stop the tape and read some comments on what you have just heard.

Now start the tape.

Poetry session: extract 1

7.29 This extract took the group up to the completion of the first draft of the first three lines, read out at the end of the extract by Wayne:

> Sirens wailing screeching roaring
> People running screaming
> The droning of the planes fly overhead

I shall comment on three aspects of the learning process in the extract: the range and quality of contributions from the special school pupils in the group; the teacher's role; and how the group organized itself.

Contributions from special school pupils

7.30   The two children from Sutton School in this group are Craig and Marcelle. Craig is quiet. He makes one contribution: when invited he suggests 'the droning of the planes'. This very apt phrase is built into the poem. Marcelle is one of the liveliest members, producing ten ideas for the poem in this extract:

> Screeching of the bombs
>
> Whistling of the bombs
>
> Screaming
>
> Whispering in the air-raid shelter
>
> People running everywhere, some frightened
>
> People everywhere in the rubble
>
> They was thinking if they'll be next. They was counting in the houses
>
> There was dogs sniffing, find people out of the rubble, see if they was still alive
>
> You heard the fire engine going by, cleaning (?) the fires out
>
> When it's finished it's started again

7.31   Marcelle makes more contributions than Wayne and Stuart, and similar amounts to Bobby and Sam, all of them pupils from Russells Hall. The group is not dominated by the mainstream pupils. On other occasions too, Marcelle was a fluent and creative contributor to group poems.

7.32   There are so many ideas suggested for this poem that only a fraction of them can be included. The richness of ideas must depend partly on the vivid resources that the group draws on. The video and interviews both have the advantage of being immediately accessible to children with limited reading ability.

The teacher's role

7.33   The first point to note is how little Chris Morris says. He makes only six contributions:

> Is someone going to write the extra sounds down?
>
> What have you got on the original list, 'cos you don't need to write it down again?
>
> What else did you see on the video?
>
> You got enough ideas down there to begin with?
>
> What were you saying?
>
> Is that how you want to start the poem then?

7.34 The amount of pupil talk is as striking as the lack of teacher talk. Are the two linked? Does Chris's minimal input enable the pupils to contribute more extensively? My guess is that it does, but that the quantity and quality of pupil talk depends on other factors as well. One is the way the task has been organized and the resource material that pupils can draw on. Another is the fact that the pupils at Russells Hall had been used to this style of working for some time, although to the pupils from Sutton School, it was new.

7.35 The second point to note is that Chris's input is limited to helping pupils to manage the task. He does not offer any ideas for the poem, nor does he try to lead the pupils towards any particular ideas. But he is not the group's sole 'organizer': teacher and pupils manage the task together.

How the group organizes itself

7.36 Between them, Chris and the pupils keep the work moving in a relatively unobtrusive fashion. Sam, who is the scribe at this stage, takes the lead role. Looking at what the 'chair' of the group does gives us an insight into the skills involved in effective group work like this. I noted six headings:

(a) Gathering contributions; sometimes this is directed at the group as a whole, sometimes at individuals.

(b) Shifting topic; e.g. 'Right feelings now' and 'Shall we put the words and that into order?'

(c) Maintaining focus; e.g. 'That's when they're going to evacuation. We're doing one about the blitz.'

(d) Recapping/summarizing; e.g. 'Let's see what sounds and that we've got so far.'

(e) Evaluating progress; e.g. 'You got enough ideas down there to begin with?'

(f) Identifying and assigning tasks; e.g. 'Is someone going to write the extra sounds down?'

Now start the tape again.

Poetry session: extract 2

7.37 In this extract the group has nearly completed the first draft of the poem, and they need to find an ending. Two alternatives emerge: either the bombing starts up again, or the all-clear sounds. The idea that the bombing might restart is potentially a powerful ending, suggesting the unforgiving relentlessness of war. Marcelle had already proposed the idea in extract 1 ('When it's finished it's started again'). Wayne suggests 'The siren wails. The nightmare starts again.' This is a final line from another poem he had seen, the strength of which has been emphasized in an earlier lesson when endings had been discussed. Sam and Bobby both wanted a gentler, more hopeful outcome. Bobby offers the solution: 'We could have both, 'cos the planes could go away and then five hours later or summit, it starts again'. That this is accepted without demur indicates the extent of the group's commitment to a joint outcome. The solution then gives rise to a new problem: how to link the departure and return of the bombers. And this yields new ideas. Marcelle's image of 'one little boy left' is poignant, and it shows how she can integrate ideas from different sources. When she talks about 'the big boy who didn't want to go', she is alluding to a video of the evacuation that the group had seen on another day.

7.38   This episode shows productive conflict at work in a group that is committed to a joint outcome. Note that Chris does not arbitrate, or impose a solution. He simply points to the problem. The conflict leads into new possibilities, new creations, and the deployment of unused resources. Note that in this case, unlike the research I discussed earlier, there is no right answer towards which the group is working.

Now start the tape again.

Question-writing session: extract 2

7.39   In this extract, Dipak from Sutton asks a question which reveals a presupposition which is challenged:

> DIPAK: Ah yeah. Next one. What places did you go to. When [?] you joined the war. What place did you go to?
>
> [?]: Which places?
>
> DIPAK: What places did you go to?
>
> [?]: Did anybody interview Mr Hill?
>
> SCOTT: Yeah, we did.
>
> CLAIRE: Did he, was he in an aeroplane or not? Was he home guard or what?
>
> SCOTT: He was only just a kid.
>
> TINA: [*reading*] Were there times when you thought you was going to die?
>
> CLAIRE: Oh! [*responding to Scott*]
>
> SCOTT: He isn't that old.
>
> CLAIRE: Well I didn't know.

7.40   This episode shows how learning opportunities can arise in a task which encourages children to reveal their ideas and beliefs about the subject in question. Note that they are not being asked directly to say what they know about the war, but they have deployed their understanding in order to complete the task. They have to make what they know public, and this opens it to challenge, debate and modification. In this instance the matter is resolved within the group. In others, a question allows the group to identify an area of real uncertainty. The question of Mr Hill's age during the war is resolved for Claire in this extract, but you'll hear in the next extract that Dipak still believes that he was old enough to carry a gun. You will also hear how the matter is resolved for Dipak. The pupils in this group act as resources for each other in two senses: they share what they know; and by doing so, they point to areas of uncertainty. They discover what they know, what they do not know, and what they might need to rethink.

7.41 You may also have noticed that the questions they pose cover the factual (What places did you go to?) and the emotional (What was the most terrifying bit during the war for you?). The personal experience conveyed by the interviews gives pupils not just insights into the details of life during the war, but also what it felt like. This personal involvement is a powerful means of access to history. Later in the tape you will hear pupils discussing this.

Now start the tape again.

Question-writing session: extract 3

7.42 I have transcribed the whole of this extract to help the analysis.

TINA: What did you say? [*To Dipak*]

DIPAK: Forgot now. [?] [...] What place did you travel to in the war?

TINA: That's like where did you live during the war and things?

TINA: Think of any Claire?

IAIN: What food did you eat?

TINA: We've already asked that one. We've got it. It says ...

DIPAK: Did you have any guns on you, anything like that?

TINA: It says here.

CLAIRE: Did you get injured in the war?

TINA: [*Reading*] What sort of food was rationing, could you tell us the most typical meal. I've got that.

JOHN: Did you have any clothes?

DIPAK: Shut up. Clothes!

JOHN: No I was thinking [...] rations.

TINA: Iain your turn the same questions. Think, think.

CLAIRE: Did you ever get injured?

DIPAK: Did you travel [...] Did you carry any guns with you? Anything like that?

JOHN [?]: Weapons.

DIPAK: Yeah, did you carry any weapons on you?

TINA: Did your family carry any weapons with them?

DIPAK: Him. Did he carry any?

TINA: I don't think he would.

CLAIRE: Oh 'cos he's only a kid then.

TINA: So shall I say 'Did your family carry any weapons with them?'?

DIPAK: Yeah.

CLAIRE: Arms or anything.

Chris Morris and Linda Whittall: working on the recordings

Stan Hill

Linda with Marcelle holding the microphone

Vereena Ranford: transcribing a tape

First-hand evidence

Artwork from an integrated project

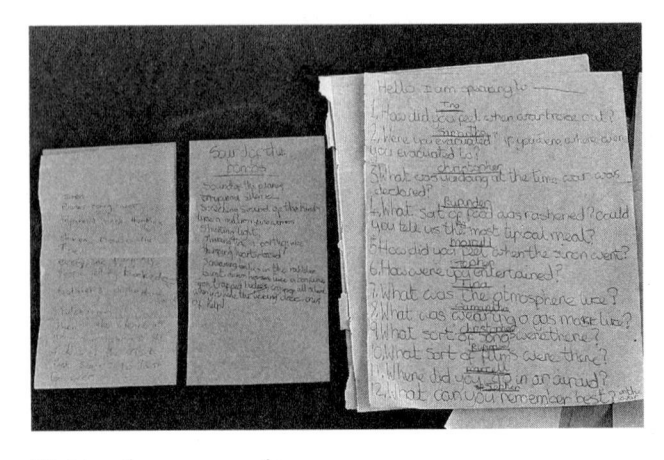

Writing for a range of purposes

DIPAK: Did you ever have a chance to see the pictures? What films?

[?]: Cinema.

DIPAK: At the cinema.

[?]: Were there any cinemas there? Were there any cinemas round him?

[?]: No they was all closed or something. Closed down.

DIPAK: Was it closed?

[?]: It was closed down, weren't they?

TINA: I'm sure they was all closed down.

7.43   Much of this extract is devoted to forming questions which are suggested by Dipak. (Remember, he is one of the group from the special school.) The first concerns travel. Dipak still appears to think of Mr Hill as an adult. It seems that Tina rewords the question to allow for Mr Hill's actual age at the time. Dipak's question about guns is also modified, and in this case, Tina and Claire make the reasons clear. Dipak has now sorted out his misconception. His third question produces valuable uncertainty. The group is led to think carefully about whether there were cinemas, and if so, were they open?

7.44   Here we see the way in which the group supports and extends Dipak's ideas. Bruner might refer to this as 'scaffolding'. But the talk is mutually beneficial. Dipak offers ideas; the other members of the group extend and modify them in the light of their understanding. Dipak gains from having his ideas taken up and developed. The group as a whole gains from his supply of ideas.

7.45   John, also from the special school, makes one of his two contributions to the list of possible questions during the whole session: 'Clothes'. In this extract the idea is dismissed by Dipak and gets no further. But note that John is able to hint at what he intended: a question about rationing clothes. In the next extract, you will hear John's point retrieved.

Now start the tape again.

Question-writing session: extract 4

7.46   Here is how the episode about John's clothes point goes:

TINA: [*Unclear*]

SCOTT: So what have we got, er gotta think.

[?]: [*Unclear*]

[?]: Something about clothes. I can't remember now.

SCOTT: Clothes.

CLAIRE: Did they ration clothes?

SCOTT: Did they ration clothes?

JOHN: Yeah that was it.

Now John's idea has been included in the list of questions. Note how the group takes on the task of constructing a question from John's idea. This gives him the satisfaction of seeing his idea taken seriously and an insight into how questions can be formulated. The contrast between the group's response here and Dipak's dismissive attitude earlier is stark.

7.47 The episode raises a number of questions. How much does the wide span of ability in the group help to support John? Would a group of less skilled pupils offer John the same learning opportunities? Perhaps he might have been more forthcoming in a group without other such competent members. Or perhaps he would be just as reserved and his idea would have been left undeveloped. What should be the role of the teacher in such a group? What would you have done when Dipak dismissed John's idea? Would you have intervened? Immediately or later? What could have been done to encourage Dipak to respond more openly by exploring what John meant?

Summary

7.48 We have seen examples of collaborative learning achieving all four of the functions I discussed earlier:

(a) making thinking explicit: in all the episodes you have listened to;

(b) supporting ideas: in the way the group scaffolds for John and Dipak;

(c) ideas in conflict: in the problem of how to end the poem and the debate over Mr Hill's age;

(d) exploratory thinking: in the collecting of ideas for the poem and in the discussions about the details of life during the war.

7.49 You should play the rest of the tape straight through to the end. It deals with what the children learned about the War, and what they learned about each other. Since I am not going to discuss this part of the tape in the unit, it will help if you make notes on this part of the tape. As you listen think about:

(a) What made history accessible for the children? Did the children from the special school need different materials or methods to give them access to the Second World War?

(b) How does the project illustrate the diversification of lessons I discussed in Section 6?

(c) How did the views of the children and their teachers change during the project? In what ways are the views of the children and their teachers about the project similar and different?

Now start the tape again and listen to the end.

BARRIERS TO COLLABORATION

7.50 Introducing collaborative learning methods of the kind I have illustrated in the Russells Hall/Sutton project involves changing the groundrules and power structure of classrooms. Such a change is potentially a major challenge to everyone involved, teachers and pupils alike. It creates new roles, relationships and expectations. So we should not be surprised to find resistance and opposition to the introduction of collaboration in classrooms, especially where the change in method is very substantial. At Russells Hall, the mainstream schoolchildren were already well used to active learning in small groups. This may have been an important factor in the success of the project.

7.51 Helen Cowie and Jean Ruddock (1990) interviewed a large number of teachers about their attitudes to collaborative group work, and revealed in these teachers 'widespread anxiety about their own capacity to deal with the challenge ... Even teachers who are committed to group work may face criticism and hostility from sceptical colleagues' (Cowie and Ruddock, 1990, p. 248). The potential level of hostility can be seen in the views expressed in this extract from a discussion between three secondary science teachers who have just heard a recording of a group of pupils working collaboratively:

> DAVID: They were genuinely searching for things. And the kids were actually prepared to put themselves on the line with one another.
> PETER: I don't understand that. That will not happen in a formal classroom situation, putting kids round a table and saying, 'let's perform ... '.
> DAVID: You wouldn't do that. You would prepare people for it and use it as part of a programme. It is not an end in itself. It is a means to an end. It's a technique and the sort of discussion that is going on there, why shouldn't it go on in a small group in science? How do we know that doesn't go on if we don't listen?
> PETER: You take a typical group where you have 24 kids where you split them up into six groups of four. Now in any typical group that I teach, there are at least five or six disruptive kids in that unit. I would doubt that you would get any serious conversation going on in that class.
> JERRY: [*tentatively*] We actually have tried this method in Science. We find a problem and we sit in groups and get them to work out how to do an experiment ...
> PETER: There's nothing wrong with them discussing but if it's a planned experiment the written exercise is done on an individual basis.
> JERRY: I don't see anything wrong with them discussing.
> PETER: In the old fashioned terminology, it is cribbing. Yes, cribbing! In an examination, you might just as well say, 'Instead of having a formal exam, just sit next to each other'.

(Cowie and Ruddock, 1990, pp. 249–50)

Activity 16 Collaboration or cribbing?

(a) What are Peter's grounds for opposing collaborative learning?

(b) What is your response to these arguments?

7.52 Peter's opposition appears to rest on a combination of firmly held beliefs about how learning should take place, and his experience of teaching. His first concern is that the loss of control implied by small-group work would lead to disruption. But is it possible that the level of disruption he experiences is caused by the way he currently teaches, and would reduce with small-group work? How could this idea be broached and tested out? How might a learning support teacher interested in collaborative learning handle this situation? Peter also holds the view that children should be able to learn and demonstrate their learning on their own. Cooperation amounts to cheating. In case you think this view is isolated, bear in mind that, as of 1991, the Open University still will not accept jointly submitted assignments in any of its courses (although this does not mean that the University is opposed to collaboration in learning – far from it). One response to Peter's cribbing argument would be to point to the many adult intellectual activities, including most scientific research, which are pursued collaboratively.

7.53 Pupils too can sometimes actively resist collaborative learning. Phillida Salmon and Hilary Claire (1984) followed the efforts of a small group of secondary teachers in some detail as they tried to introduce collaboration into their classrooms. One of the teachers, Islay, worked with a bottom stream Year 10 social studies group in a school with low expectations of such children and a traditional, teacher-led curriculum. The group was pursuing an examination course with a syllabus devised by the school, and approved by their examination board. Islay's class were seen as resistant pupils, and they felt alienated from school. Although the introduction of collaborative methods helped to increase the solidarity of the class, and developed good social relationships, the extent of actual collaborative learning was very limited. Despite encouragement to write together, written work remained individual. The class did not see discussion as 'real work', and much preferred to be told what to do. Salmon and Claire argue that a number of factors contributed to these attitudes. First was the salience of the exam. Second, and more important, the messages about learning that underpinned Islay's work were contradicted by everything else in her class's school experience. These pupils had developed an image in the school as immature, incompetent and unable to take responsibility. They had no experience of learning independently. Taking the initiative in lessons in a way that was sanctioned by the teacher was a new venture for them. They saw learning as something that involved coercion.

7.54 Salmon and Claire concluded that five factors are important for the success of collaborative learning:

- positive feelings towards the school among pupils;
- positive feelings towards the teacher as a working partner, not an impersonal authority;
- a view of peers as a resource for each other;
- willingness by pupils to take responsibility for their own work;
- self-esteem in sufficient degree for pupils to trust their own capacities as learners.

7.55 The absence of many of these features in Islay's class derived, Salmon and Claire argue, from the way in which their school defined learning and their status as pupils. Thus the development of collaboration in the classroom depends to some extent on the existence of whole-school policies and practices to support it. That is an issue we shall take up in Unit 16.

COLLABORATIVE LEARNING ENVIRONMENTS

7.56 How might the work of the Russells Hall/Sutton project be applied in other classrooms? If a teacher wished to foster collaboration of the kind we heard in Cassette Programme 2, what should be done? During the project the teachers designed collaborative tasks for the children. They were not highly directed and the children could respond in many ways, but they were set up on the teachers' initiative and the children were expected to work as a group to complete the task. It is tempting to conclude that the job entails designing and setting up teacher-initiated learning tasks that will encourage children to collaborate. Yet, as Salmon and Claire showed, collaborative and supportive relationships do not come 'naturally' to all pupils. We have not examined the learning background of the pupils at Russells Hall in any detail, nor the ethos of the school. Salmon and Claire's work suggests that this may have been important in accounting for the effective collaboration we observed. Some observations by Rachel Roberts (1988) provide further insight into the circumstances in which collaboration may and may not occur. She recorded a group of three Year 10 boys in the 'MLD Unit' of a comprehensive school working on a task which involved interpreting a temperature chart taken from a published maths scheme:

> There is some attempt at plotting the graph but this falters very quickly as all students have difficulty with the axes, and quickly give up. Their approach to failure is very much to go on, without spending a great deal of time on trying different strategies. For example, at different times they express frustration:
>
> PATRICK: There are two times in the day when the temperature was 5.5°. What were they? ... I haven't got the foggiest, let's turn over.

MARTIN: 11:50. This is pissing me off ... Can't get it right.

PATRICK: Oh no, I've gone past it. It can't be. I'm going to leave that bit.

[...]

Robert and Patrick seem to understand the task, and work in silence. Martin becomes completely disengaged from the task, having only focused on it whilst I was present. He constantly states that he is bored ...

The main feature of the way in which these students worked was their lack of interaction, I felt. They seemed unable to work in a collaborative manner. Listening to the whole tape – over an hour's worth of material – I found only one example [...] of an attempt to explain and answer. Elicitation of help was confined to Martin, who simply wanted to be told what the answer was, and where he should put it. These were not kindly received; even when they were less exploitative:

MARTIN: We've got to put it in the 5s up here, haven't we?

ROBERT: You twit, you berk!

MARTIN: I ain't bothered, I don't care. The next one goes up in fucking 5s, don't it?

[*No response*]

They even seem suspicious of working together:

ROBERT: I won't be with you all the time, you know Patrick, do your own dirty work.

They seem to feel that this is cheating. There is no evidence of the hypothetical mode which Barnes (1976) feels is directly linked with success in collaborative work and the use of language as an aid to learning.

This was all rather disheartening. However, at the end of the tape, once the students had worked for as long as I had expected, there occurred a very interesting exchange [...] which illustrates a completely different mode. Martin cut his finger earlier in the week, and had required a tetanus jab:

MARTIN: Can I get a plaster? To put it there like that.

ROBERT: You'll need another one to wrap round the top of it.

MARTIN: I cut that, an' I see red stuff with the blue.

PATRICK: It was a vein.

MARTIN: Yeah!

PATRICK: You'd be dead.

MARTIN: No I wouldn't.

ROBERT: You said you could see the vein, you never said you cut the vein ... 'Ere, Rachel, if you cut the vein in your hand, would you be dead?

MARTIN: No, your finger.

PATRICK: You've got to tie something round it.

RACHEL [teacher]: Yeah, you'd have to stop the bleeding.

ROBERT: Yeah, but if you cut it down you'd be ...

[conversation continues]

This section differs significantly from previous 'on-task' discussion. Students are using hypothetical constructions, involving outside help in a constructive manner. [...] They are eager to pursue their own points and clear up ambiguities. They do not seem content with the simple 'yes you do, no you don't' format which they used during the maths session. All contribute to the discussion, with characteristically longer utterances.

(Roberts, 1988, pp. 10–14)

7.57 So these boys do not lack the skills to learn collaboratively. Why then didn't they use them in the maths lesson? Rachel Roberts argues that they have come to expect learning tasks which are imposed and meaningless: 'they have no ownership over their own learning'. Their objective in such tasks is not to understand, but to finish. They depend on teachers to tell them what to do and how they are doing. 'Teachers perceive that they are very demanding of time, and so devise structured individual programmes based on reinforcement of basic skills'. It is these boys' commitment to their task, or the lack of it, that may be critical in motivating their collaboration, or not. Thus 'group work' of itself is not a guarantee of collaboration. Other factors are involved, but what are they? Salmon and Claire's work points to pupil and teacher attitudes and the learning environment of schools. These ideas seem at first glance to be rather diffuse and in need of closer analysis. In the final reading for Unit 6/7, Susan Hart discusses the way in which some primary teachers have tried to establish classroom environments in which children can learn and deploy collaborative skills. We shall see that this goes well beyond 'group work'.

Activity 17 Beyond group work

Now read 'Collaborative classrooms', by Susan Hart (Reader 1, Chapter 1). You will find that the chapter is quite detailed, though the arguments are very clear. In the first two sections Susan Hart shows how collaboration involved much more than group work in the primary classrooms she studied. Note here the main differences between the kind of collaboration she expected to find, and what she in fact found. In Section 3 she describes the nature of the collaborative environments she observed. First she looks at how the teachers created a 'self-supporting framework' which enabled children to work independently of the teacher; second, she analyses how the teachers helped pupils to make good use of the opportunities for collaboration that this framework provided. You may find it useful to take notes under these headings.

TV4 *The Write to Choose*

7.58   Under this punning title of admittedly dodgy quality, TV Programme 4 provides some practical illustrations of many of the issues that I have discussed in this and earlier sections. We selected one area of the curriculum – writing – and one age range – primary – to show how some of the teachers in two schools:

- developed collaborative learning environments of the kind discussed by Susan Hart;
- exploited the possibilities of collaborative work to foster children's writing;
- encouraged children to be active learners, drawing on their own knowledge and understanding of the writing process.

7.59   You will see work in four classrooms. In the first, we visit Mary Heath's Year 3 class at Rice Trevor Lower School, Bedfordshire. When we filmed, Mary's class spent a morning on a visit to Bromham Hall, a big rambling house in the village. In the afternoon the class began to work on that experience.

7.60   The other three classrooms are all in one school: Sir Thomas Abney Primary School, in the London Borough of Hackney. We see:

- Kathy Kelly, the head of the school, working with a Year 6 class who are making information books for younger children;
- Jasbir Thethi, working with her Year 1 class;
- Kevin Glassar, working with one of the classes in the school's unit for children with speech and language difficulties.

Before the programme

Mary Heath's class

7.61   In this part of the programme we have sought to give an impression of a classroom in which a teacher has developed a collaborative learning environment. You will see a number of short episodes and examples of pupils' work.

Episode 1   Introduction from George
7.62   The programme begins with some images of the visit, and a piece of factual writing by George. George had only recently joined the class, having moved from another school. He needed a great deal of support and confidence building as a writer. The piece you see is a final draft done on the word processor. Figure 14 shows an example of George's first draft writing, in response to a request from Mary to write about the day we filmed.

Episode 2   Getting Matthew started
7.63   Mary works with Matthew, who is able to write with some confidence, but finds it difficult to find a starting point. Watch how Mary

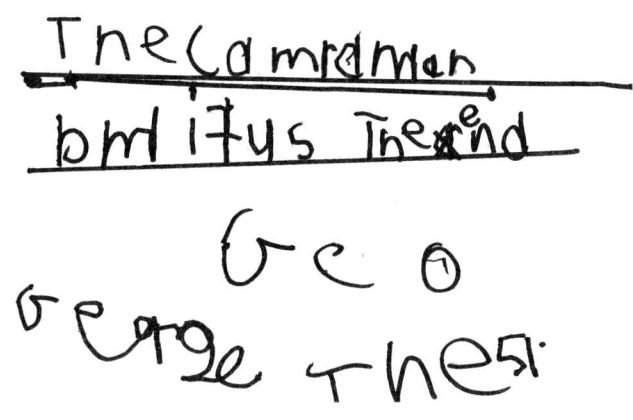

Figure 14 George's first draft writing

tries to establish his own interests and involves another member of the class. Compare this episode with what Susan Hart says under 'Using children as resources'.

Episode 3   Natalie and Victoria not working on the visit
7.64   Natalie and Victoria develop a piece of work that did not come from the visit. Giving pupils control over their learning can involve their controlling the organization of their time. Natalie and Victoria are self-assured, confident writers. Notice the way they collaborate and the clear sense of purpose and involvement in their work. You may be surprised that we should include this episode, since it obviously does not involve pupils who are experiencing difficulties. But if we want to create classrooms that respond to diversity, then we need to look at what all pupils are doing, not just those who are less competent and confident. One of the arguments in favour of classroom environments that encourage independent learning is that the teacher is freed to give individual support to pupils. How do you react to this argument? Compare this episode with Susan Hart's comments under the heading 'Control'.

Episode 4   A brief consultation
7.65   Natalie (a different Natalie!) consults Jessica about what she plans to do. Mary considers this an important indication of the ethos she tries to build up: 'this reflects a shared interest in the thinking about the work. It is rare for me to see these classroom processes, which I have to rely on'. Here is an example of the fleeting collaboration Susan Hart describes in Section 2 of her chapter.

Episode 5   Christopher: purpose and audience
7.66   Christopher is one of two pupils in the class who receives help from a learning support teacher who visits the school to work with children who are delayed in their reading and writing development. Watch how Mary helps Christopher to see a purpose for writing, and how another pupil provides a ready-made audience. Compare this with Susan Hart's comments under the heading 'Understanding purposes for collaboration'.

Episode 6 Jenny's reflections on dying

7.67 This piece of writing emerged from a visit to the grave of Mary Rice Trevor, who lived at Bromham Hall, and whose name is preserved in the school's name. The choice of topic arose from Jenny alone. We use this piece to show the place that redrafting has in Mary's class, and the way that Jenny works at the 'secretarial' aspects of her writing: spelling, grammar and punctuation, in order to express her meaning.

Episode 7 Emily feeling left out

7.68 Emily missed the morning visit. She uses writing to record and reflect on how she felt in the afternoon. Note the very personal nature of her writing, and her willingness to share it with the rest of the class. Mary invited her to read it out, but she was free to refuse. What does this episode tell us about the classroom environment? Compare this with Susan Hart's comments under the heading 'Supportive relationships'.

Kathy Kelly: producing books for infants

7.69 In this lesson we concentrate on one group: Joshua, Darren and Ibby, all of whom experience considerable difficulties in writing. Together they are producing a book on frogs – their current passion – designed for younger children. Watch here for:

- the way in which the task gives them choices to make, and control over what they do. Compare this with Susan Hart's comments on 'Commitment';
- the separation of planning of the content of the book and the production of a polished final draft;
- the sense of audience and purpose in the work;
- the motivation the task gives this group to work on basic skills such as spelling. Notice how the task provides a meaningful context for the practice of these skills.

Jasbir Thethi: developing confidence from the start

7.70 In this brief visit to a reception class, we see the way in which pupils can develop a sense of control over their own writing from the start. In this session, Jasbir provides a combination of models of writing in a shared writing session and encouragement to pupils to explore writing for themselves. She aims to give all pupils a sense that they can make meanings on paper – the prerequisite for becoming a confident writer. Each pupil develops their writing individually. The programme shows examples of children in this class using what resources they have to make meanings, and extending the range of their resources, developing towards adult forms. Jasbir offers her pupils models of writing, but the way they incorporate these experiences varies from one individual to the next.

Kevin Glassar: a writing workshop

7.71 This is a class in which all the pupils have Statements. They have all transferred from other primary schools to the Unit at Sir Thomas Abney and have been identified as having speech and language difficulties. They receive a combination of class teaching with a favourable teacher–pupil ratio, and speech therapy.

7.72 The lesson we filmed is a 'writing workshop'. In the first part of the lesson, Kevin writes for the class. In the second part, the pupils write for themselves. They have a completely free choice of topic. Kevin helps them to choose by listing three possible topics and then selecting one. Kevin is concerned to help his pupils to expand their writing: 'They tend to adopt what I would call avoidance strategies to furthering the development of their writing. I am trying to get beyond what I consider to be stereotypic or formulaic writing, and lots of short repetition work'. He is also concerned to foster their independence as writers and to encourage them to use each other as resources. In the first part of the lesson Kevin invites questions about his own piece of writing. At the end of the lesson we see one pupil, Rose, reading out her work and answering questions about it.

7.73 This lesson is only part of the process of helping these pupils to become more confident writers. Kevin comments: 'Once they get into the habit of this way of working they can go and read their stories to a friend, they can redraft it and publish it as part of an overall programme of written work'. Sheila Eimermann, the classroom assistant in this class, has noticed the progress the children have already made: 'I can remember in the past there were kids queueing up with things, and that doesn't happen now. I've worked with special needs children for sixteen years, and writing has always been the most difficult thing for them ... so I can see a tremendous difference'.

Activity 18 *The Write to Choose*

Now watch TV5. If you can record the programme to watch it again you will get more out of it. Here is a summary of points to concentrate on:

- in Mary Heath's class, the collaborative learning environment;
- in Kathy Kelly's lesson, the nature of the task, how it gives the group a meaningful context for their writing and the way they collaborate;
- in Jasbir Theti's lesson, the way these young learners develop a sense of confidence in their ability as writers;
- in Kevin Glassar's lesson, how he gives the children some control over their work and helps them to see a purpose in writing.

SUMMARY

7.78 Collaborative learning comes in many different forms and is associated with many different educational goals, some of them conflicting. Some forms of collaborative learning reproduce authority relationships between teacher and pupil in the relationships between pupils; others seek to change it.

7.79 Collaboration can help children to learn by encouraging them to make their thinking explicit, by providing support for children so that they can do things together that they could not do alone, by bringing competing ideas in conflict, and by fostering exploratory thinking. These processes can benefit all children, including those who have been identified as having learning difficulties.

7.80 Collaborative learning methods may be opposed by teachers and pupils alike if they present a threat to established relationships in classrooms, if they conflict with firmly held educational values, or if they challenge pupils' and teachers' views of how learning should happen.

7.81 The successful use of collaborative learning methods depends in part on children being personally committed to the tasks they undertake in the classroom, and having some control over how they undertake them.

7.82 Primary classrooms where collaboration is an important part of life are not just characterized by teacher-led group work. Children collaborate over individual tasks, which they have defined themselves, and the collaboration may be only short term. Teachers in such classrooms aim to create a self-supporting framework to allow children to work independently of their teacher, and they teach children how to use this framework to best effect.

8 INVESTIGATIONS

Views on in-class support and withdrawal

8.1 In this option you investigate the attitudes of a small group of teachers towards in-class support and withdrawal teaching. Choose either three or four teachers who you will interview. These could be mainstream teachers who have experience of using in-class support and withdrawal teaching for children who experience difficulties, or learning support teachers. Your aim is to explore their experiences of in-class support and withdrawal teaching and their views on the respective merits of the two approaches. Each interview should normally last no more than 30 minutes. You should ask the interviewees:

(a) to give basic details of the job they do;

(b) to describe in broad terms the way in which learning support is provided in their school;

(c) to describe some of their experiences of in-class support and withdrawal, including those which have been successful and unsuccessful from their point of view;

(d) to give their views on the strengths and weaknesses of the examples they describe;

(e) to compare in general terms the benefits and disadvantages of the two approaches.

Difficulties with texts

8.2 In this option you investigate the difficulties created by a small number of texts. Gather the texts used in the course of one school day by one pupil known to you who experiences difficulties in learning.

(a) Analyse some of these texts in terms of the features of school texts discussed in Section 4, and assess the potential difficulties they may pose for the pupil you have chosen.

(b) Examine any work done by the pupil in response to the texts in the form of writing, drawings, completed worksheets, tape-recordings, etc. to see what evidence it provides about the pupil's understanding of the texts.

(c) Investigate the meaning of some of the texts for the pupil you have chosen by discussing them with him or her. What does your chosen pupil understand and think about the text and its subject matter?

Classroom dialogue

8.3 In this option you investigate potential difficulties created by the way language is used in the classroom.

(a) Tape record a maximum of ten minutes of teacher–pupil dialogue. If you are a teacher this could be yourself, or it could be a teacher you know who is willing to be recorded. You could record a whole-class discussion, a discussion with a small group, or a one-to-one conversation.

(b) Transcribe the recording.

(c) Select and analyse some short extracts from the dialogue in terms of the conversational power of the participants, the groundrules assumed by the teacher, and the degree to which these are shared by the pupil(s).

8.4 Warning: getting a good recording of classroom dialogue is difficult, especially if it is a whole-class session. It also takes a long time to prepare an accurate transcript, and ten minutes of dialogue turns into many pages of transcript.

Collaboration

8.5 In this option you investigate collaborative learning with a group of children which includes at least one child who has been identified as having learning difficulties.

(a) Select a lesson in which some small-group work will take place, and choose one group which will include at least one child identified as having learning difficulties by the class teacher (which could be yourself). Choose an activity where you expect there to be talk between pupils.

(b) Tape record and transcribe a maximum of ten minutes of the dialogue between pupils.

(c) Analyse short extracts from this dialogue in terms of the issues raised in Section 7 concerning the learning processes in collaborative activity and the problems of and barriers to collaboration.

USING THE MATERIAL

8.6 We hope that the material in this double unit will prove useful in INSET activities in primary, secondary and special schools. You may find that the two TV programmes and the audio-cassette band offer especially useful resources for whole-school or department staff development.

8.7 If a school is planning to review its policy on learning support, then the analysis of the arguments for learning support and withdrawal, the factors affecting in-class support and the distinction between the individual and whole curriculum approaches, all in Section 3, may provide a framework for analysing current practice.

8.8 Schools wishing to review and enhance the accessibility of their written resources may find it useful to look at them, and how they are used, in terms of the analysis in Section 4.

8.9 Schools and departments that would like to (a) make their curriculum accessible to a wider diversity of pupils, (b) introduce more open-ended activities which give pupils more involvement in their own learning, and (c) foster collaborative learning, may find TV3 and Cassette programme 2 useful stimuli for discussion and development.

8.10 Schools and teachers who wish to review the learning environment of their classrooms may find that Reader 1, Chapter 1 offers a useful beginning.

8.11 None of the material should be seen as offering a model to be reproduced precisely in other classrooms. The TV and audio-cassette programmes, reader chapters and unit can help by raising issues and prompting collaborative reflection on current practice.

REFERENCES

AHMED, A. (ed.) (1987) *Better Mathematics: a curriculum development study*, London, HMSO.

ARONSON, E. (1978) *The Jigsaw Classroom*, Beverly Hills, CA, Sage.

BARNES, D. (1976) *From Communication to Curriculum*, Harmondsworth, Penguin.

BARNES, D. (1988) 'The politics of oracy', in MACCLURE, M., PHILLIPS, T. and WILKINSON, A. (eds) *Oracy Matters*, Milton Keynes, Open University Press.

BENNETT, N., DESFORGES, C., COCKBURN, A. and WILKINSON, B. (1984) *The Quality of Pupil Learning Experience*, London, Lawrence Erlbaum Associates.

BERNSTEIN, B. (1971) *Class, Codes and Control, Volume 1*, London, Routledge and Kegan Paul.

BEST, R. (1987) 'Pupil perspectives on remedial education: an empirical comment', *International Journal of Adolescence and Youth*, **1**, pp. 69–97.

BEST, R. (1991) 'Support teaching in a comprehensive school: some reflections on recent experience', *Support for Learning*, **6** (1), pp. 27–31.

BOOTH, T. (1987) 'Perceptions of consultancy', in BOOTH, T., POTTS, P. and SWANN, W. (eds) *Preventing Difficulties in Learning*, Oxford, Basil Blackwell.

BOOTH, T., POTTS, P. and SWANN, W. (eds) (1987) *Preventing Difficulties in Learning*, Oxford, Basil Blackwell.

BRIDGES, D. (1979) *Education, Democracy and Discussion*, Windsor, NFER.

BRUNER, J. S. (1985) 'Vygotsky: a historical and conceptual perspective', in WERTSCH, J. V. (ed.) *Culture, Communication and Cognition: Vygotskian perspectives*, Cambridge, Cambridge University Press.

CAVEN, M. (1987) 'A market-place for learning', in BOOTH, T., POTTS, P. and SWANN, W. (eds) *Preventing Difficulties in Learning*, Oxford, Basil Blackwell.

CHERRINGTON, V. (1990) 'Developing contexts for writing non-narrative', in WADE, B. (ed.) *Reading for Real*, Milton Keynes, Open University Press.

CLUNIES-ROSS, L. and WIMHURST, S. (1983) *The Right Balance: provision for slow learners in secondary schools*, Windsor, NFER/Nelson.

COWIE, H. and RUDDOCK, J. (1990) 'Learning from one another: the challenge', in FOOT, H. C., MORGAN, M. J. and SHUTE, R. H. (eds) *Children Helping Children*, London, Wiley.

CURRIE, H. (1990) 'Making texts more readable', *British Journal of Special Education*, **17** (4), pp. 137–9.

DAVIES, L. (1980) 'The social construction of low achievement', in RAYBOULD, E. (ed.) *Helping the Low Achiever in the Secondary School*, Educational Review Occasional Publication No. 7, Birmingham, Educational Review.

DEPARTMENT OF EDUCATION AND SCIENCE (DES) (1978) *Special Educational Needs*, London, HMSO (The Warnock Report).

DEVRIES, D. and SLAVIN, R. (1978) 'Teams–Games–Tournaments: a research review', *Journal of Research and Development in Education*, 12, pp. 28–38.

DOISE, W. and MUGNY, G. (1984) *The Social Development of the Intellect*, Oxford, Pergamon Press.

DOISE, W. (1990) 'The development of individual competencies through social interaction', in FOOT, H. C., MORGAN, M. J. and SHUTE, R. H. (eds) *Children Helping Children*, London, Wiley.

DYER, C. (1988) 'Which support? An examination of the term', *Support for Learning*, 3 (1), pp. 6–11.

EDWARDS, A. D. (1980) 'Patterns of power and authority in classroom talk' in WOODS, P. (ed.) *Teacher Strategies: explorations in the sociology of the school*, London, Croom Helm.

EDWARDS, A. D. and FURLONG, V. (1978) *The Language of Teaching*, London, Heinemann.

EDWARDS, D. and MERCER, N. (1987) *Common Knowledge: the development of understanding in the classroom*, London, Methuen.

EDWARDS, J. R. (1979) *Language and Disadvantage*, London, Edward Arnold.

FLEMING, H., DADSWELL, P. and DODGSON, H. (1990) 'Reflections on the integration of children with learning difficulties into secondary mathematics classes', *Support for Learning*, 5 (4), pp. 180–5.

FLETCHER, B. C. (1985) 'Group and individual learning of junior school children on a microcomputer-based task: social or cognitive facilitation?', *Educational Review*, 37 (3), pp. 251–61.

GIPPS, C., GROSS, H. and GOLDSTEIN, H. (1987) *Warnock's Eighteen Per Cent: children with special needs in the primary school*, London, Falmer Press.

GOLBY, M. and GULLIVER, J. C. (1979) 'Whose remedies? Whose ills? A critical review of remedial education', *Journal of Curriculum Studies*, 11, pp. 137–47.

HARGREAVES, D. H. (1967) *Social Relations in a Secondary School*, London, Routledge and Kegan Paul.

HARRISON, C. (1980) *Readability in the Classroom*, Cambridge, Cambridge University Press.

HART, S. (1987) 'A lesson from humanities', in BOOTH, T., POTTS, P. and SWANN, W. (eds) *Preventing Difficulties in Learning*, Oxford, Basil Blackwell.

HART, S. (1989) 'Everest in plimsolls', in MONGON, D., HART, S., ACE, C. and RAWLINGS, A. (eds) *Improving Classroom Behaviour: new directions for teachers and pupils*, London, Cassell.

HEATH, S. B. (1982) 'Questioning at home and at school: a comparative study' in SPINDLER, G. (ed.) *Doing the Ethnography of Schooling: educational anthropology in action*, New York, Holt, Rinehart and Winston.

HOWE, A. (1988) *Expanding Horizons*, Sheffield, National Association of Teachers of English (NATE).

HUGHES, M. and COUSINS, J. (1988) 'The roots of oracy: early language at home and at school', in MACCLURE, M., PHILLIPS, T. and WILKINSON, A. (eds) *Oracy Matters*, Milton Keynes, Open University Press.

HULL, R. (1985) *The Language Gap: how classroom dialogue fails*, London, Methuen.

HULL, R. (1990) 'Some fictions of non-fiction', *Books for Keeps*, **60**, pp. 16–19.

INGRAM, J. and WORRALL, N. (1990) 'Varieties of curricular experience: backmarkers and frontrunners in the primary classroom', *British Journal of Educational Psychology*, 60, pp. 52–62.

JOHNSON, D. W. and JOHNSON, R. T. (1975) *Learning Together and Alone: cooperation, competition and individualization*, Englewood Cliffs, NJ, Prentice-Hall.

JOWETT, S., HEGARTY, S. and MOSES, D. (1988) *Joining Forces: a study of links between special and ordinary school*, Windsor, NFER-Nelson.

KYNE, P. (1987) 'The Kent face: introducing mixed-ability maths', in BOOTH, T., POTTS, P. and SWANN, W. (eds) *Preventing Difficulties in Learning*, Oxford, Basil Blackwell.

LIGHT, P. and GLACHAN, M. (1985) 'Facilitation of individual problem solving through peer interaction', *Educational Psychology*, **5**, pp. 217–26.

LUNT, I. (1987) 'Special needs in the primary school', in THOMAS, G. and FEILER, A. (eds) *Planning for Special Needs: a whole-school approach*, Oxford, Basil Blackwell.

LUNZER, E. and GARDNER, K. (eds) (1979) *The Effective Use of Reading*, London, Heinemann Educational.

LUNZER, E., GARDNER, K., DAVIES, F. and GREENE, T. (1984) *Learning from the Written Word*, Edinburgh, Oliver and Boyd.

MEHAN, H. (1979) *Learning Lessons: social organization in the classroom*, Cambridge, MA, Harvard University Press.

MONTGOMERY, D. (1990) *Children with Learning Difficulties*, London, Cassell Educational.

PERERA, K. (1984) *Children's Writing and Reading: analysing classroom language*, Oxford, Basil Blackwell.

PHINN, G. (1987) 'No language to speak of? Children writing and talking', in BOOTH, T., POTTS, P. and SWANN, W. (eds) *Preventing Difficulties in Learning*, Oxford, Basil Blackwell.

RICHMOND, R. C. and SMITH, C. J. (1990) 'Support for special needs: the class teacher's perspective', *Oxford Review of Education*, **16** (3), pp. 295–310.

ROBERTS, R. (1988) *A Study of the Linguistic Skills used by Statemented Students in Problem-solving Situations*, MA in Education, project report, School of Education, The Open University.

ROSEN, M. (1989) *Did I Hear You Write?*, London, André Deutsch.

ROSENTHAL, R. and JACOBSON, L. (1968) *Pygmalion in the Classroom*, New York, Rinehart and Winston.

SALMON, P. and CLAIRE, H. (1984) *Classroom Collaboration*, London, Routledge and Kegan Paul.

SCOTTISH EDUCATION DEPARTMENT (SED) (1978) *The Education of Pupils with Learning Difficulties in Primary and Secondary Schools in Scotland: a progress report by Her Majesty's Inspectorate*, Edinburgh, HMSO.

SNOW, C. E. (1983) 'Literacy and language: relationships during the preschool years', *Harvard Educational Review*, **53**, pp. 165–89.

STOKES, A. (1978) 'The reliability of readability formulae', *Journal of Research in Reading*, **1** (1), pp. 21–34.

TIZARD, B. and HUGHES, M. (1984) *Young Children Learning: talking and thinking at home and at school*, London, Fontana.

TOPPING, K. (1988) *The Peer Tutoring Handbook: promoting co-operative learning*, London, Croom Helm.

TOUGH, J. (1977) *The Development of Meaning*, London, George Allen and Unwin.

UPTON, G. (1989) 'Overcoming learning difficulties', in RAMASUT, A. (ed.) *Whole-school Approaches to Special Needs*, London, Falmer Press.

VYGOTSKY, L. S. (1978) *Mind in Society: the development of higher psychological processes*, Cambridge, MA, Harvard University Press.

WADE, B. (ed.) (1985) *Talking to Some Purpose*, Educational Review, Occasional Publication No. 12, Birmingham, Education Review.

WADE, B. (1990) 'Approaches to reading', in WADE, B. (ed.) *Reading for Real*, Milton Keynes, Open University Press.

WATTS, L. and NISBET, J. (1974) *Legibility in Children's Books: a review of research*, Windsor, NFER.

WELLS, G. (1985) 'Preschool literacy-related activities and success in school', in OLSON, D. R., TORRANCE, N. and HILDYARD, A. (eds) *Literacy, Language and Learning*, Cambridge, Cambridge University Press.

WELLS, G. (1986) *The Meaning Makers: children learning language and using language to learn*, Cambridge, Cambridge University Press.

WHELDALL, K. and METTEM, P. (1985) 'Behavioural peer tutoring: training 16-year-old tutors to employ the "Pause, Prompt and Praise" method with 12-year-old remedial readers', *Educational Psychology*, **5** (1), pp. 27–44.

WOODS, P. (ed.) (1980) *Pupil Strategies: explorations in the sociology of the school*, London, Croom Helm.

ACKNOWLEDGEMENTS

Grateful acknowledgement is made to the following sources for permission to use material in this unit:

Figures

Figure 2: Standard Assessment Task Teacher's Book, 1991. Schools Examinations and Assessment Council. Reproduced by permission of the Department of Education and Science; *Figure 3:* Burgess, C. V., *Burgess Competition Book 2*, 1967, University of London Press; *Figure 4.* Currie, H., 'Making texts more readable', *British Journal of Special Education*, vol. 17, no. 4, December 1990, National Council for Special Education. Reproduced by permission of the author publisher and Berkshire County Council; *Figure 5:* Hull, R., *The Language Gap:* 1985, Methuen. Reproduced by permission of International Thomson Publishing Services, Ltd.

The course team is grateful to the following schools and institutions for permission to record and reproduce classwork:

Harold Hill Community School, Romford, Essex

Watergate Special School, Newport, Isle of Wight

Tideway School, Newhaven, East Sussex

Russells Hall Junior School, Dudley, West Midlands

Sutton Special School, Dudley, West Midlands

Sir Thomas Abney Primary School, Stoke Newington, Hackney

Rice Trevor Lower School, Bromham, Bedfordshire

The Mathematics Centre, West Sussex Institute of Higher Education

APPENDIX: READABILITY FORMULAE

Both formulae given below rely on counting words and syllables. Neither of these is entirely easy to define. For practical purposes a written word can be defined as a string of characters delimited by spaces. It is not always easy to count the number of syllables in a word. Does 'remedial' have three or four syllables? There is no simple answer to such problems.

Measured readability depends on the sample of text used. Texts are not always consistent in the readability score they produce from sample to sample. A rule of thumb is to use at least three 100 word passages. If the results vary a lot, then more samples should be taken.

THE FLESCH FORMULA

This formula produces a 'reading ease score' which can then be converted into an age level. The reading ease score (RES) is calculated by the formula:

Reading ease score = 206.835 − (0.846 × sylls/100w) − (1.015 × wds/sen)

where 'sylls/100w' means syllables per 100 words, and 'wds/sen' means average number of words per sentence.

Age levels are found from this score using different formulae according to the score:

Reading Ease Score	Formula for age level
Over 70	5 − ((RES − 150)/10)
Over 60	5 − ((RES − 110)/5)
Over 50	5 − ((RES − 93)/3.33)
Under 50	5 − ((RES − 140)/6.66)

THE POWERS–SUMNER–KEARL–FORMULA

In this formula the age level is calculated directly, as follows:

Age level = 2.7971 − (0.0778 × wds/sen) + (0.0455 × syll/100w)

where 'wds/sen' means average number of words per sentence, and 'sylls/100w' means syllables per 100 words.

This formula rarely produces age levels outside the range 7–12 years, so is not suitable for many secondary school texts.

If you are planning to use a readability formula extensively, consult Harrison (1980) first.

E242: UNIT TITLES

Unit 1/2   Making Connections
Unit 3/4   Learning from Experience
Unit 5   Right from the Start
Unit 6/7   Classroom Diversity
Unit 8/9   Difference and Distinction
Unit 10   Critical Reading
Unit 11/12   Happy Memories
Unit 13   Further and Higher
Unit 14   Power in the System
Unit 15   Local Authority?
Unit 16   Learning for All